CW00725153

COMBATING TERRORISM

Saudi Arabia's Role in the War on Terror

COMBATING TERRORISM

Saudi Arabia's Role in the War on Terror

Ali S. Awadh Asseri

OXFORD

UNIVERSITY PRESS

OXFORD

UNIVERSITY PRESS

Great Clarendon Street, Oxford OX2 6DP

Oxford University Press is a department of the University of Oxford.
It furthers the University's objective of excellence in research, scholarship,
and education by publishing worldwide in

Oxford New York

Auckland Cape Town Dar es Salaam Hong Kong Karachi
Kuala Lumpur Madrid Melbourne Mexico City Nairobi
New Delhi Shanghai Taipei Toronto

with offices in

Argentina Austria Brazil Chile Czech Republic France Greece
Guatemala Hungary Italy Japan Poland Portugal Singapore
South Korea Switzerland Turkey Ukraine Vietnam

Oxford is a registered trade mark of Oxford University Press
in the UK and in certain other countries

ISBN 978-0-19-547807-5

Typeset in Adobe Garamond Pro
Printed in Pakistan by
Kagzi Printers, Karachi.
Published by
Ameena Saiyid, Oxford University Press
No. 38, Sector 15, Korangi Industrial Area, PO Box 8214
Karachi-74900, Pakistan.

Contents

Preface

This book is an effort to place in perspective the highly emotive and controversial subject of terrorism, including its theoretical dimensions and practical manifestations. The Kingdom of Saudi Arabia, like several other countries of the Muslim world and the West, has been a victim of terrorism. Unlike many others, however, the Saudi counter-terrorism strategy is making a huge difference on the ground. What is it in the Saudi strategy that has contributed to its relative success? What lessons does it have for other Muslim countries in particular and the world in general trying to combat the wave of international terrorism? The book answers these questions, and discusses some cases in the Muslim world where counter-terrorism strategies on the lines of the Saudi experience have produced meaningful results. Moreover, an attempt has been made to address some broader issues, including whether religion is acting as a means or an end in the contemporary wave of terrorism, what the true spirit of Islam is as a religion of peace, and finally, what the international community needs to do to control terrorism in the short-term and eliminate it in the long-term.

However, in so far as various conceptual and contextual issues relating to terrorism are concerned, the articulation of an alternative Saudi or Muslim perspective is extremely important. I attempt to accomplish this task substantively in the first four chapters which help to clarify numerous critical issues concerning the subject and are not necessarily in conflict with mainstream Western opinions on the matter.

Having served for over eight years as Saudi ambassador to Pakistan, I see this brotherly country suffering profusely at the hands of terrorists. The idea of writing this book occurred to me as I witnessed the unfurling horror of terrorist violence in Pakistan, the region, and the world. Having lived in the midst of terrorism for many years, I was extremely conscious of the urgent need to formulate an effective and long-term strategy to combat the scourge.

I started delving into the history and dynamics of terrorism and how the world, through centuries, had been adversely impacted by it, as well as how it had endeavoured to deal with it. The more I researched the subject, the more my interest increased and so did my commitment to making a credible contribution to this priority concern of the international community.

Obviously, I looked towards my own country that had already been a victim of terrorism in the past. I also studied the mechanism and the means that the Saudi government had adopted to deal with the menace and became increasingly conscious of the wisdom that guided it. I realized that terrorism is a phenomenon that cannot be bombed out of the face of the world. It is a battle of winning over the hearts and minds of the people—the perpetrators as well as those who suffer as a consequence of an act of terrorism.

While there was substantial reason to combat the scourge of extreme behaviour, there was also a need to look at other factors that may have contributed to the evolution of this violent pattern. In fact, it was a case of looking beyond the boundaries of the obvious. Of looking at multi-faceted deprivations that a large percentage of the world population, particularly in the developing world including the Muslim world, suffered from, and those who did not have the opportunity to send their children to school to be educated and who, consequently, became willing targets of deviant minds. It was a case of looking at those segments of our population that were undernourished and underprivileged, and of showing a greater level of sensitivity to those who could not afford social and health care for their families, and who continually suffered for reasons beyond their control such as alarming child and female mortality rates. There was also the problem of increasing unemployment that sowed the seeds of disenchantment and frustration. I realized that discrimination, of whatever nature, bred discontentment and by not tackling the social, political and cultural problems facing a large segment of the world population urgently, we had only aggravated the causes that contributed to extreme behaviour and action. It was in fighting obscurantism that we might find our salvation, and in caring for humanity and helping them solve their problems that one could look for the means to combat terrorism.

That is when the wisdom of the Saudi strategy dawned upon me. While force always remained an alternative, here was a case of finding a solution by laying stress on the cardinal elements of prevention, cure and care. Instead of showering a rain of bullets on the perpetrators and the affected without discrimination, thus encouraging others to embrace the cause of terrorism out of sympathy, here was an effort to educate and influence the mindset of people so that they could be rationally driven away from terrorism and its devastating manifestations.

I hope that, by undertaking this effort, I am able to make a meaningful contribution to the evolution of a sustaining and credible international strategy to combat the crime of terrorism. The world, irrespective of its adherence to multiple religions, beliefs and socio-political systems, should stand united in its resolve to fight this battle, and aim at winning over a significant segment of the world population that has been infected by the germs of terrorism through continual neglect and disregard for the root causes that have contributed to the emergence of this menace as a formidable challenge today.

In this humble effort, I stand beholden to the contribution of my colleagues, my family and friends without whose support I would not have been able to finish this book. I am thankful to HRH Prince Mohammad bin Naif, Assistant to the Minister of Interior for Security Affairs, Government of Saudi Arabia for providing me with the relevant material as well as guidance vide numerous meetings regarding the Saudi anti-terrorism strategy.

I am also grateful to my wife Aishah and children, Abdulaziz, Hussam and Faisal, for showing immense patience with me when I was absent for prolonged periods working at the office. I am also grateful to my teachers and friends for encouraging and guiding me through various stages of executing the project.

I would like to particularly mention Dr Ishtiaq Ahmad, who read the manuscript and came up with extremely useful suggestions and additions. I would also like to mention my brother Raoof Hasan who worked with me for long hours and guided me through various phases of doing the requisite research for the arduous project. I would always remain indebted for his contribution and effort.

This book is an academic work and is the outcome of my dissertation for my Master's programme. The contents of this book exclusively represent my personal views and do not, in any manner, reflect the viewpoint of the Saudi government.

Terrorism is a scourge that has to be fought and eliminated. I hope this book would contribute, in some meaningful measure, in evolving a strategy to defeat the forces of terror and make the world a safe place for all people without discrimination on the basis of caste, colour, creed or other affiliation. We all belong to this world and it is everyone's right to live in peace and harmony. I dedicate the book to this dream and hope that it may soon come true.

ALI S. AWADH ASSERI
Islamabad

1

Terrorism in Theory

Terrorism is indeed the world's most prevalent phenomenon today. There seems to be no escaping from it, at least in the near future. It has haunted us for ages and it will continue to haunt us if we fail to evolve an international consensus on its causes, nature, scope, implications, and solution. Without developing a sound understanding of terrorism, no strategy to combat it can succeed. However, the principal problem in developing such an understanding or realizing an international consensus on terrorism is our tendency to simplify issues, whereas terrorism is an extremely complex issue involving a lot of controversy. Perhaps that is why the world has, so far, failed to evolve a universally accepted definition of terrorism. As a starting point, therefore, what we need is to place the subject of terrorism in its proper theoretical and conceptual framework, and to see whether it is possible to at least create its workable or functional definition.

This chapter makes use of important theoretical perspectives on terrorism available in contemporary Western literature, however, pinpointing some of its fundamental flaws. There are issues that are overplayed or over-emphasized by Western writers on the subject, either intentionally or inadvertently. This necessitates a critical review of the established opinions on what terrorism is, for which purpose it is undertaken, what its eventual goals are, and how it relates to other forms of politically motivated violence. To start with, the question of a single theoretical definition of terrorism has haunted the human mind for decades, but all efforts in that direction have failed to evolve a consensus. The horrific connotations of the word 'terrorism' and the feelings of revulsion it evokes are the reasons behind a vast array of theoretical definitions available on the subject. The problem in defining terrorism pertains to labelling, because 'terrorist' is a description that has almost never been voluntarily adopted by any individual or group,[1] what to speak of a state entity that, under international law, has the right to use force to ensure self-defence and preserve territorial integrity, however, with some pre-conditions!

Various countries define the term according to their own beliefs and to support their own national interests. International organizations craft definitions to promote the interests of their member-states, while academics engaged in this exercise are also quite often subject to their own political points of view. Since terrorism implies the killing or maiming of innocent people, no country wants to be accused of supporting terrorism or harbouring terrorist groups. No country, however, wants what it deems to be a legitimate use of force to be considered terrorism. This is the paradox that has perplexed the human mind endeavouring to define terrorism. That is why all the definitions of terrorism crafted by states, state institutions and international governmental organizations mention only non-state individuals and groups, and do not include states as perpetrators of terrorism.

PROBLEM OF DEFINING TERRORISM

It was specific state practice in late eighteenth century Europe deliberately aimed at intimidating citizens and to prevent anarchy and maintain order that introduced the word 'terrorism'. To be more precise, the term entered Western vocabulary during the French Revolution, derived from Jacobin rule under Maximilien Robespierre during 1793–94, known as the 'Reign of Terror'. Over time, however, 'terrorism' came to be essentially associated with militant activities of private groups and organizations. This is the presumption in almost all of the current attempts by states, or state institutions, especially Western, to define terrorism. For instance, the US Department of Defence defines terrorism as 'the calculated use of violence or the threat of violence to inculcate fear, intended to coerce or to intimidate governments or societies in the pursuit of goals that are generally political, religious, or ideological'.[2] The British government defines terrorism as 'the use of threat, for the purpose of advancing a political, religious, or ideological course of action, of serious violence against any person or property'. According to the German government, terrorism is 'the enduringly conducted struggle for political goals, which are intended to be achieved by means of assaults on the life and property of other persons, especially by means of severe crime'.[3]

Scholarly definitions of terrorism also abound. For instance, Bruce Hoffman defines terrorism as 'the deliberate creation and exploitation of fear through violence, or the threat of violence in the pursuit of political change'.[4] Alex P. Schmid offers a more comprehensive definition. According to him, terrorism is:

> an anxiety-inspiring method of repeated violent action, employed by (semi-) clandestine individual, group or state actors, for idiosyncratic, criminal or political reasons, whereby—in contrast to assassination—the direct targets of violence are not the main targets. The immediate human victims of violence are generally chosen randomly (targets of opportunity) or selectively (representative or symbolic targets) from a target population, and serve as message generators. Threat- and violence-based communication processes between terrorist (organization), (imperilled) victims, and main targets are used to manipulate the main target (audience[s]), turning it into a target of terror, a target of demands, or a target of attention, depending on whether intimidation, coercion, or propaganda is primarily sought.[5]

However, no governmental or academic attempt so far to define terrorism has achieved international consensus. The same has been the case with international organizations, which have mostly tried to identify some acts of militancy perpetrated by individuals or groups as 'terrorist'. For instance, the League of Nations Convention of 1937 had defined terrorism as 'all criminal acts directed against a state and intended or calculated to create a state of terror in the minds of particular persons, or a group of persons, or the general public'.[6] Thomas Mockaitis says:

> The United Nations has struggled for years to agree on a common definition of terrorism. Two issues consistently block consensus: inclusion of acts of terror by states and the insistence by some members that any definition must distinguish between the acts of terrorists and those whom they consider 'freedom fighters'. Many also express the justifiable concern that efforts to combat terrorism may erode human rights that the organization has consistently fought to uphold. Faced with this seemingly insurmountable impasse, the organization continues to expand the legal framework for combating terrorism.[7]

A United Nations General Assembly Resolution of 1999 pertaining to measures for eliminating international terrorism offered the following to define the acts of 'terror': all 'criminal acts intended or calculated to provoke a state of terror in the general public, a group of persons or particular persons for political purposes are, in any circumstance, unjustifiable, whatever the considerations of a political, philosophical, ideological, racial, ethnic, religious or other nature that may be invoked to justify them'.[8] Currently, twelve international conventions define and outlaw specific terrorist acts ranging from hijacking to bombing.[9] The UN Security Council Resolution 1377, while elaborating upon such acts, described international terrorism as 'one of the most serious threats to international peace and security in the twenty-first century' and 'a challenge to all states and all humanity'.[10] Useful as this approach may be in combating terrorism, it does not offer much guidance in understanding terrorism or its root causes.

All of these attempts to, theoretically and conceptually, define terrorism by academics, state entities or organizations representing state-governments are problematic. As argued before, state and organizational definitions presume that terrorism can only be committed by either individuals or groups of people. What is implicit in this assumption is that the use of violence by 'sub-national groups' is illegal. In the state's view, only the state has the right to use force, meaning the state has a monopoly on the legitimate use of violence. However, those who differ with such rationale wonder whether all use of violence by non-state actors is equally unjustifiable. Some definitions of terrorism, such as the ones offered by international organizations, avoid a reference to the perpetrators of terrorism, fearing that if they do so, then the word 'state' would also have to be mentioned. The definitions offered by the US, British or German governments are equally problematic, since they fail to distinguish between terrorism and other forms of politically motivated violence such as war and guerrilla warfare.

In fact, a closer look at the current definitions of terrorism reveals that almost all of them tend to 'classify an act as terrorism based on three broad criteria: target, weapon and perpetrator'. Virtually all experts and officials agree that indiscriminate attacks on civilians constitute terrorism. They also consider use of certain weapons deemed illegitimate by the international community as terrorism. Finally, most experts and officials assess the legitimacy, goals, and objectives of the perpetrators in deciding whether or not to declare their actions 'terrorism'. Unfortunately, each criterion and any combination of the three again present a serious problem: terrorists do deliberately attack civilians but so did all belligerents in the Second World War. Strategic bombing is aimed specifically at breaking enemy morale by destroying heavily populated cities and killing their inhabitants.[11] The recent 'Shock and Awe' policy during the Iraq War was, likewise, aimed at terrorizing the supporters of the former Baathist regime of Saddam Hussain. Similarly, quite often, the sort of weapons that terrorist organizations use, even including chemical agents, are employed by states engaged in warfare.

TERRORISM AND WARFARE

We can safely conclude from the preceding discussion that boundaries between terrorism and warfare are really blurred. One way of understanding terrorism is to distinguish it from all other forms of politically motivated acts of violence, which terrorism is. War, guerrilla warfare, and insurgency are all politically motivated acts of violence. However, they differ from terrorism in the sense that, theoretically speaking, the perpetrators involved in each make a clear distinction between armed and unarmed civilians. Unarmed civilians are not to be attacked in a war, guerrilla war, or insurgency. Yet the ground reality is that, in each of these cases, unarmed civilians do often become victims of warfare. When this happens during a war, as it has frequently during the ongoing wars in Iraq and Afghanistan, it is termed as 'collateral damage' by the state entities or international coalitions involved. The argument that is offered in defence of this strategy is that, since the terrorist entity is hiding its military assets in a civilian area and using civilians as 'human shields', a military strike, particularly an air assault, would naturally result in some civilian casualties. This implies that while fighting terrorism militarily, it is difficult to avoid collateral damage.[12]

Just as in the case of war, during a guerrilla war, quite often the perpetrators, the weapons used, and the victims show enormous similarity with the same in terrorism. Gone are the days when guerrilla warfare was confined only to rural areas. Since the late 1960s, we have seen an increasing wave of urban guerrilla war, during which even if an attack is meant against a military target in a city, unarmed civilians turn out to be its principal casualty. The psychological effect that results from an urban guerrilla campaign is also a reality. Even during the time of the classical guerrilla warfare, when it was a phenomenon confined to the countryside, acts of terrorism did accompany the traditional guerrilla violence specifically targeting the standing army of the state the guerrillas were at war with. This occurred most often during the initial stages of the guerrilla campaign, as the guerrilla organization intended, through acts of terrorism, to trigger an over-reaction from the state concerned so that a greater number of people sympathetic to their cause from among the general populations could be recruited for guerrilla operations.

Thus, terrorism may be termed as violence in peacetime—and perhaps that is why its impact is so spectacular and it gets so much attention—but it is difficult to distinguish it from all other acts of politically motivated violence. On the other hand, mob violence is also a politically motivated act of violence, but it can be distinguished from terrorism because it does not take place deliberately and is not organized and employed systematically as is the case with terrorism.[13]

Like guerrilla warfare, insurgency as a form of modern conflict may or may not involve terrorism. Thomas Mockaitis argues:

Because of the stigma attached to the term, threatened states often refer to insurgents as terrorists, even though insurgent goals and methods differ markedly from those of terrorist organizations. Calling insurgents 'terrorists' for propaganda purposes adds to the confusion surrounding the nature of both forms of conflict. Insurgency is an organized movement to take over a state from within through a combination of propaganda, guerrilla warfare, and terrorism. Although insurgents have embraced a variety of broad ideologies, they have decidedly focused political goals. They seek political power within a nation state by overthrowing an established government. Insurgents feed on grievances within a population, persuading those who feel their government does not meet their basic needs that it must be replaced with one that does. Insurgents make use of terror, but they do so selectively. Since their success depends, in large measure, on winning the support or at least the acceptance of the general population, they seek to avoid actions that alienate people. They target government facilities, assassinate officials, and murder ordinary people who aid the authorities, but they generally avoid inflicting mass casualties. Insurgent terror can also provoke the government into using force so indiscriminately as to further alienate disaffected people and drive them into the arms of the insurgents.[14]

Given that, according to Mockaitis,

a clear distinction between terror and guerrilla warfare, both of which insurgents employ, must be made. Guerrilla warfare involves irregular forces operating out of uniform and in loose formations. Historically, guerrillas have attacked small regular military units, isolated outposts, police, and government paramilitary forces. Guerrillas used hit-and-run tactics, striking when opportunity arose and then melting back into the general population. Unlike guerrilla operations, terrorist attacks target the general population. Terror can be used by a variety of actors: nation states, insurgent movements, criminal organizations and terrorist groups. An effective operational definition must clearly distinguish between these actors. The greatest confusion in the current struggle lies in distinguishing between terror employed by insurgents and terror employed by organizations whose goals are so idealistic as to be virtually unattainable. It is for this second group that the term 'terrorist' should be reserved.[15]

TERRORIST VERSUS FREEDOM FIGHTER

Terrorism is certainly a value-laden concept. 'One man's terrorist is another man's freedom fighter' is a popular dictum that, in fact, sums up the highly subjective and judgemental nature of terrorism as a political concept. If a country, a group of people or an individual sympathizes with the cause of a non-state organization, and if this non-state organization happens to deliberately commit a violent act against unarmed civilians, this will not be a terrorist act in the eyes of the sympathizers. However, the state entity against which such an act is committed will certainly call it an act of terrorism. What happens in the process is that, consequently, a blame game begins in which each side accuses the other of being terrorists while positing itself to be either fighting for freedom, as non-state actors often do, or trying to safeguard its territorial integrity, as state actors mostly do. There is, then, no end to this blame game, and no way, therefore, to objectively understand what terrorism is.

In a sense, employing the dictum of 'one man's terrorist is another man's freedom fighter' amounts to simplifying a complex issue such as terrorism, and any objective assessment of the subject has to explore the grey zone between freedom fight and terrorism. It is possible that, during the course of a freedom fight, some acts of terrorism occur. It is also possible that a terrorist organization may be motivated by the goal of freedom. Charles Townshend argues: 'On the historical record, those who have adopted a purely terrorist strategy have not been successful liberators. Conversely, the liberators were not pure or absolute terrorists'.[16] In other words, it is possible that a freedom movement may employ terrorist tactics, and it is also possible that a terrorist movement is guided by the goal of freedom.

Thus, according to Leonard Weinberg,

> by saying that 'one man's terrorist is another man's freedom fighter', the observer is simply confusing the goal with the activity. Almost everyone concedes that terrorism is a tactic, one involving the threat or use of violence. If this is true, there is, in principle, no reason why this tactic cannot be used by groups seeking to achieve any number of goals and objectives, including a fight for freedom or national liberation.[17]

The 'one man's terrorist is another man's freedom fighter' argument serves merely to 'undercut the natural human antipathy for terrorist methods, and permit terrorist propaganda far more credence than it deserves'.[18] 'Critics of this strong statement,' according to Mockaitis,

> will argue that it dismisses the legitimacy of some insurgent goals. This concern may be addressed by separating ends and means. Certain heinous acts can be condemned no matter what causes they serve. International conventions against the use of torture make no exception based on the intentions of the perpetrators. Suicide bombing deserves the same condemnation.[19]

Hasan-Askari Rizvi adds to the terrorist versus freedom fighter debate while pointing out a dilemma that arises when, an abstract articulation of terrorism is applied to an incident in its political and historical context. Much, therefore, depends upon how a specific incident is interpreted. As historical and political narratives vary, the use of violence may be viewed as 'justified' and 'understandable' by some in a specific context, while others interpret it as terrorism that cannot be condoned. Given that, each movement will have to be examined with reference to its historical and political context and the goal it pursues. Some of these movements may be pursuing well-recognized goals like elimination of racial discrimination, national rights and the right of self-determination. These factors have to be taken into account before passing judgement.[20]

Hasan-Askari further argues:

The methods employed by these movements should also be reviewed. Do they rely exclusively on violence, or is it coupled with non-violent strategies? If they resort to violence, the key questions are its frequency, methodology, and the primary target. If violent methods involving killing and destruction are used as the primary method and the civilians are targeted systematically and persistently, such a movement is vulnerable to the charge of using terrorism. Furthermore, we should also take into account the policies of the challenged authorities towards these movements. The states and the political authorities often use the coercive apparatus in a persistent and systematic manner to suppress dissident, nationalist and liberation movements. The criterion of terrorism should be applied to both sides rather than condoning the actions of the state authorities. If one side adopts terrorist methods as a matter of policy, the other side is likely to respond in the same manner.[21]

Finally, almost all terrorism experts agree that organized non-state terrorism is not necessarily always motivated by 'progressive' or 'good' causes, i.e. changing a status quo perceived to be unjust. Terrorist violence has been conducted by groups that want to retain or restore systems of racial supremacy such as the Ku Klux Klan in the United States, or to promote the establishment or re-establishment of a right-wing dictatorship in the name of neo-Nazi or neo-Fascist ideas. In addition, some Latin American countries in the recent past, from Colombia to El Salvador to Chile, have been sites of 'death squads', bands of killers (frequently off-duty soldiers or police officers in civilian dress) who wage assassination campaigns against land reformers, union organizers, members of the Catholic clergy, and others identified with promoting the interests of the poor. In Northern Ireland, loyalist paramilitary organizations have repeatedly carried out terrorist attacks with the goal of maintaining the region's link to the United Kingdom.[22]

TOWARDS A FUNCTIONAL DEFINITION

Despite such complexities, it is important to develop a rational understanding of terrorism. As Adrian Guelke points out, understanding terrorism in general presents the problem that the term 'terrorism' entails an absolutist judgment that seems quite incompatible with the retention of any element of empathy for its perpetrators, or the situation that spawned them. The absence of empathy is a very evident feature of the literature on terrorism. It is most clearly reflected in a relative lack of interest in the explanations that those who are identified as terrorists have to offer for their actions. It is not difficult to suggest why. In the first place, no writer seeking to establish his or her credentials in the field of terrorism would wish to provide, or even appear to provide, any rationalization for an act of terrorism. In the second place, there is the problem of fitting the explanations that terrorists give into the framework provided by the concept of terrorism. There are ample reasons why the influence of terrorism on the modern world is worth examining, not in spite of, but in the light of, the barriers that exist to understanding the term. Furthermore, an elucidation of the issue of terrorism has a wider relevance to an understanding of both the nature of the world and of the age in which we live.[23]

Walter Laqueur argues for a rational understanding of terrorism, but in a slightly different way. According to him,

'with all the misunderstandings, deliberate and involuntary, on the subject of terrorism, it is still true that people reasonably familiar with the terrorist phenomenon will agree 90 per cent of the time about what terrorism is, just as they will agree on democracy or nationalism or other concepts. In fact, terrorism is an unmistakable phenomenon, even if the search for a scientific, all-comprehensive definition is a futile enterprise'. Any definition beyond 'the systematic use of murder, injury, and destruction, or the threat of such acts, aimed at achieving political ends' will result in controversy, and arguments will go on endlessly. The position of the student of terrorism is not unlike that of a physician dealing with a disease, the exact causes of which remain unknown to this day, or a drug of which it is not known how precisely it functions. But this will not prevent him from diagnosing the disease, or from prescribing the drugs that are applicable.[24]

Just because it is difficult to arrive at a universally accepted definition of terrorism, or an understanding that is largely acceptable by the international community, it should not discourage us from placing the subject in an academic perspective. In fact, Muslim scholars need to explore logical and rational explanations of terrorism to an even greater degree than their Western counterparts, since the story has so far predominantly been told by the latter, and quite often in a distorted manner. It is unfortunate that the Muslim scholarly discourse on the subject has thus far been based more on emotion and conspiracy theories. Probably, that is why a section of the Western scholars, particularly Bruce Hoffman, have succeeded in portraying religion as a goal rather than a means while discussing terrorist motivations pertaining to the contemporary wave of international terrorism. The fact, however, is that terrorism committed by deviant organizations in the Muslim world is an outcome of their misinterpretation or misuse of religious scripture, just as it has been the case with successive millenarian cults in the history of Judaism and Christianity.

We shall engage in this debate in greater detail in the next two chapters. In so far as the above-discussed theoretical formulations of terrorism are concerned, it is clear that we need a functional rather than a theoretical definition of the problem. As Mockaitis argues,

> the place to begin in fashioning a functional definition is not with terrorism but with terror, a weapon that can be used by a variety of actors. Terror, unlike most weapons, aims not merely to destroy enemy combatants, but to spread fear among the general population.[25]

'Terror', as one commentator observes, 'is a theatre. Its real targets are not the innocent victims, but the spectators'.[26]

> Those who watch consist of an audience in the community under attack and an audience in the community from which the terrorists come. To the public in the targeted country, terrorists say: "See, no matter how powerful you may be, we can hit you whenever and wherever we choose"! To their own supporters they proclaim: "We are not powerless. We can deal decisive blows against our enemies". Contrary to one popular myth, terrorist attacks are never completely arbitrary. Those who use terror select targets less for their military value than for their symbolic significance. They choose buildings or landmarks that represent power, pride, or economic strength. They kill people to send a message to the group those people represent.[27]

Almost all the definitions make a common reference to the psychological element. The academic and legal definitions identify terrorism as a type of violence (or threat of violence) intended to achieve a psychological effect. Or, in other words, the immediate target or victim of a terrorist attack is only part of an operation whose main aim is to change the thinking and often the behaviour of some audience. Apart from the psychological aspect, there is general consensus about some other principal elements of terrorism: that it is a politically motivated form of violence, that it is undertaken in a deliberate and organized manner, and that it specifically targets unarmed civilians. Some Western scholars do try to underplay or altogether ignore the political motivation, especially when it comes to terrorism committed by deviant individuals and groups in the world of Islam. However, over time, even in Western scholarship, there is greater acceptance of terrorism's political dimension. The fact that a number of the Muslim world's conflicts, such as Palestine and Kashmir, have remained unresolved decades after the UN Security Council passed resolutions for their just settlement, provides a fundamental political context for terrorism by deviant individuals or groups in the world of Islam.

Thus, just because a particular argument on the causes of terrorism is being articulated and reiterated by a section of Western scholars does not mean it is entirely true. In fact, the very complex nature of the subject of terrorism implies that there has to be multiplicity and diversity in its explanation. In other words, it is possible that while discussing terrorism, or any of its important aspects, each argument may have a counter-argument. For example, state-sponsored terrorism is generally explained as a situation in which a state supports a non-state actor conducting terrorist activities in another state. However, this is only partly true as there may be instances when a state supports another state suppressing its own people. Consider another example: one of the justifications offered by non-state actors engaged in terrorist acts is that they are just responding to terrorist acts by the state. In this context, a counter-argument is that if terrorism by non-state actors is really a reaction to state terrorism, then why have most of the recent acts of terrorism by non-state actors occurred in Western democracies where citizens have all possible avenues for peaceful political expression? The debate does not stop here since the above counter-argument can be further countered by arguing that, in so far as the causes of contemporary terrorism are concerned, they may not necessarily pertain to the domestic political system of a country, but may be essentially linked to its foreign policy.

Likewise, we can expect the debate about defining terrorism to continue reflecting a variety of perspectives. To sum up the above discussion, even if a theoretical definition of terrorism lacks international consensus, at least its main elements and attributes are generally accepted. Accordingly, terrorism is an organized, deliberate and politically motivated act of violence targeting unarmed civilians with the purpose of spreading fear in a targeted audience. The main dispute over the definition of terrorism remains on identifying the culprits, which in almost all the existing definitions of terrorism offered by governments, academics, and international organizations are presumed to be non-state actors. Since states have a monopoly over the use of force under international law, they will always be reluctant to include the word 'state' in the section of terrorism definition identifying various perpetrators of terrorism. To overcome such problems, we can contextualize the definition and explanation of terrorism on a case-to-case basis.

NOTES

1. Charles Townshend, *Terrorism: A Very Short Introduction* (Oxford: Oxford University Press, 2002), p. 3.

2. *Department of Defence Dictionary of Military and Associated Terms*, Joint Publication 1–02 (Washington, DC: DOD, 2002), p. 443.

3. Alex Schmid, 'The Response Problem as a Definition Problem,' in *Terrorism and Political Violence*, Vol. 4, No. 4 (1992), pp. 8–9.

4. Bruce Hoffman, *Inside Terrorism* (New York: Columbia University Press, 1999).

5. Alex Schmid, et al., *Political Terrorism* (New Jersey: Transaction, 1988), p. 28.

6. Amy Zalman, 'Definitions of Terrorism' About.com. Available from http://terrorism.about.com/od/whatisterroris1/ss/DefineTerrorism_2.htm, accessed on 10 May 2008.

7. Thomas R. Mockaitis, *The 'New' Terrorism: Myth and Reality* (Westport, Conn.: Pentagon Press, 2007), p. 2.

8. Adopted by the UN General Assembly on 17 December 1999, 54/126/1999.

9. Leslie Palti, 'Combating Terrorism while Protecting Human Right,' *UN Chronicle*, Vol. XLI (4 November 2004).

10. Adopted by the UN Security Council at its 4413th meeting on 12 November 2001. S/RES/1377/2001.

11. Mockaitis, op. cit., p. 1.

12. Ishtiaq Ahmad, 'Simplifying a Complex Issue: The Problem in Understanding Terrorism,' paper presented at conference on 'Terrorism and Extremism: Social-Psychological Perspectives,' National Institute of Psychology, Quaid-i-Azam University, Islamabad, 15–17 October 2008.

13. Ibid.

14. Mockaitis, op. cit., p. 6.

15. Ibid., p. 5.

16. Townshend, op. cit., p. 26.

17. Leonard Weinberg, *Global Terrorism: A Beginner's Guide* (Oxford: Oneworld Publications, 2006), p. 2.

18. Christopher Harmon, *Terrorism Today* (London: Frank Cass, 1995), p. 147.

19. Mockaitis, op. cit., p. 16.

20. Hasan-Askari Rizvi, 'Theoretical Formulations on Terrorism,' in Institute of Regional Studies, *Global Terrorism: Genesis, Implications, Remedial and Counter-Measures* (Islamabad: PanGraphics, 2006), pp. 3–4 and 9–10.

21. Ibid.

22. Weinberg, op. cit., p. 8.

23. Adrian Guelke, *The Age of Terrorism and the International Political System* (New York: St. Martin's Press, 1995), p. 17.

24. Walter Laqueur, *No End to War: Terrorism in the Twenty-First Century* (New York: The Continuum International Publishing Group, 2003), p. 238.

25. Mockaitis, op. cit., p. 4.

26. David K. Shipler, *Arab and Jew: Wounded Spirits in a Promised Land* (New York: Penguin, 1987), p. 84.

27. Mockaitis, op. cit.

2

Terrorism in Practice

The theoretical formulations of terrorism as discussed before bring to the fore an important fact, which is equally applicable to the practical side of terrorism. It is that, while analysing terrorism, whether in theory or in practice, we should stay away from generalizations, monolithic perceptions, and singular explanations. Terrorism is such a complex subject that any discussion about its history, causes, purposes, goals, and forms—the focus of this chapter—will be incomplete, even misleading, if it overlooks the specific context and the circumstances, historical or contemporary, in which a particular instance of terrorism occurs. As pointed out at the beginning of the previous chapter, contemporary Western literature on terrorism is particularly afflicted with this problem. It is also worth mentioning here that the history of terrorism, its goals and purposes, causes and religious manifestations, are all inter-related subjects. For instance, the issue of religious terrorism will find reference in a discussion about the history of terrorism as well as the long-term goals of terrorism, and will not necessarily be confined to the last section exclusively meant for analysing it. In terrorism studies, it is difficult to avoid overlapping as any discussion about its manifestations and implications is directly linked with its origins and root causes. So is the case with almost every facet of the subject.

PURPOSES AND GOALS OF TERRORISM

Terrorism is an activity that has some immediate purposes and some long-term goals. Almost all the leading works on terrorism discuss the purposes and goals of terrorism. Weinberg has attempted to summarize them. According to him, as for purposes of terrorism, the first one is simply to terrify: the perpetrators of terrorist acts often hope to create a generalized sense of anxiety and fear among the public. If people become terrified, they may become immobilized and incapable of mounting a coherent response to the dangers they confront. Thus, people who become direct victims of terrorist violence are only acting as a means to intimidate a wider public audience. It is this multiplier psychological effect of terrorism that makes it a more serious act of politically motivated violence as compared to other forms of such violence, including civil war, guerrilla warfare or even war. Terrorists choose targets and actions to maximize the psychological impact on a society or a government. Their goal is to create a situation in which a government will change its policies to avoid further bloodshed or disruption. For these reasons, terrorists often choose methods of mass destruction such as bombing. They are also prone to targeting transportation or other such crowded places to increase anxiety and fear among people. Terrorists aim for maximum media coverage as it magnifies the terrorist act by spreading fear among a mass audience and giving attention to the terrorist cause.[1]

According to Weinberg, a second purpose motivating those who carry out terrorist attacks is attention or publicity for whatever cause they claim to embody. Previously obscure causes, or previously unknown groups, achieve instant celebrity through the mass media when a terrorist attack is shown to a live television audience.

A third purpose is to provoke an over-reaction by the authorities so that the terrorist entity can win more recruits from among an aggrieved population sympathetic to their cause, but unwilling to adopt terrorist means to achieve it.

Finally, terrorist groups commit especially dramatic or lethal attacks in order to polarize the situation and make a compromise settlement between two (or more) contending sides harder to achieve. Atrocities may be used to prevent moderate forces from reaching an agreement. Or, if an agreement appears to be in the immediate offing, terrorists may act as 'spoilers' by sabotaging peace negotiations and re-inflaming a troubled situation.[2]

In so far as the long-term goals of organizations employing terrorist tactics are concerned, writes Weinberg, these include revolutionary, ethno-nationalistic and separatist, religious and reactionary. Individuals and groups of people who do not possess the political power to change state policies they view as intolerable usually commit acts of terrorism. Terrorists often justify their acts on ideological or religious grounds arguing that they are responding to a greater wrong, or promoting a greater good. Before the collapse of the Soviet empire in 1989 and the subsequent disintegration of the Soviet Union itself in 1991, the world abounded with groups willing to use terrorism to bring about revolutionary social, economic and political change in the name of Communism or Socialism. Latin America was most often their venue. Argentina, Brazil, Uruguay, Colombia, and Peru had substantial 'urban guerrilla' groups that sought to bring an end to the economic exploitation of workers and peasants and replace the prevailing political order with one more compatible with their socialist principles. Japan and the highly industrialized Western democracies also had a substantial number of revolutionary terrorist organizations.[3]

According to Weinberg, ethno-nationalist and separatist terrorists are motivated by the goal of national independence, the creation of independent states carved from territories that were previously under the control or part of some other country. The Tamil Tigers in Sri Lanka, the Basque Homeland and Liberty (ETA: Euskadi Ta Askatasuna) in Spain, and the Irish Republican Army (IRA) are examples of ethno-nationalist groups seeking independence from existing countries through committing acts of terrorism. Reactionary groups, such as the Ku Klux Klan in the United States, have also used terror tactics to preserve a status quo suiting the majority population.[4] Religiously motivated terrorism is quite an old phenomenon. However, in recent decades, it seems to have dominated the global terrorist scene.

According to Louise Richardson,

Terrorists are sub-state actors who violently target non-combatants to communicate a political message to a third party. Terrorists are neither crazy nor amoral. They come from all parts of the world. They come from many walks of life. They fight for a range of different causes. Some have support from the communities from which they come while some do not. They range in size from a handful of Corsican nationalists to thousands of armed Tamils. Some are fighting for the same goals that have motivated wars for centuries, such as control over national territory. Some are trying to overthrow the state system itself. They come from all religious traditions and from none. One thing they do have in common: they are weaker than those they oppose.[5]

Whatever the immediate purposes and broader goals an organization may have, what history tells us is that terrorism has never been an effective political strategy. Whether terrorism is adopted as a tool for changing the status quo, or preserving it, it has never succeeded. Some organizations such as the African National Congress (ANC) may have adopted terrorism as part of their overall political strategy to end apartheid in South Africa, and may have eventually succeeded in their mission, but terrorism was only a tiny part of their long struggle spanning decades. Similarly, it was only after the Irish Republican Army (IRA) abandoned terrorism and agreed to de-militarize itself that the real path to a viable political accommodation in Northern Ireland was eventually paved. There is hardly any example in world history when an organized group of people exclusively practised terrorism and succeeded in achieving its political goal. Al-Qaeda is one such organization. Be it the terrorist acts of 11 September 2001 in the United States, or the 1998 bombings of two US embassies in East Africa, or the sequence of bombings in Saudi Arabia—almost all the instances implicating al-Qaeda make it crystal clear that the terrorist network, whenever it strikes, aims mostly at unarmed civilians. Thus, it engages in pure and simple terrorism whose casualties are both non-Muslims and fellow Muslims. The end result of such rampant terrorism can be foreseen in the sense that this will not only lead to a massive public reaction against al-Qaeda and its affiliates in the Muslim world, but also encourage all Muslim states to collaborate more closely with the rest of the world, East and West alike, to combat the al-Qaeda-led wave of global terrorism. For this, however, there is a precondition: that all the regional conflicts where Muslim people happen to be at the receiving end are resolved urgently and in a just and fair manner. Their continuing existence provides the political context for the deviant individuals and organizations in the world of Islam to engage in terrorist activities.

TERRORISM IN THE HISTORICAL PERSPECTIVE

Terrorism is not a new phenomenon. In some respects, what is known as terrorism in contemporary jargon predates by millennia the modern term used to describe it. This is not to say that the act of terrorism has remained static. In fact, as the difficulties involved in defining it reflect, terrorism has evolved considerably over the years. It may be that it has retained some of the same characteristics that have historically typified it. A definitive ascertainment of when it was first used may be difficult. What we call terrorism today traces its roots back at least some 2,000 years. Moreover, today's terrorism, in some respects, has come full circle as many of its contemporary practitioners are motivated by religious convictions—something that drove many of their earliest predecessors. It has also, in the generally accepted usage of the word, often possessed a political dimension. This has coloured much of the discourse surrounding terrorism—a phenomenon that, according to Paul Pillar, is 'a challenge to be managed, not solved'.[6]

The history of terrorism is as old as the history of religion itself. In fact, until the end of the nineteenth century, religion provided the only justification for terrorism. From the beginning of the nineteenth century up to the 1980s, however, religious terrorism was overshadowed by anarchist, socialist revolutionary, counter-revolutionary, anti-colonial and ethno-nationalist terrorism. These included anti-colonial and post-colonial movements for national liberation in the shape of ethno-nationalist terrorism, and right wing and left wing terrorism.[7] Religion became a far more popular means for terrorism in the post-Cold War era as old ideologies were discredited by the collapse of the Soviet Union and communist ideology. Samuel P. Huntington's 1993 'clash of civilizations' thesis placed religion at the heart of regional and global conflicts in the post-Cold War period.[8]

The religious roots of terrorism can be traced back to the Sicarii—a Jewish Zealots group that was active during the Roman occupation of first century Middle East. The famous weapon of the Sicarii, from which they also derived their name, was the sica (the short dagger which literally means 'dagger men'). The weapon was used to murder those (mainly Jews) who were deemed apostate, and thus, selected for execution. Such killings usually took place in daylight and in front of witnesses and were meant to send a message to the Roman authorities and those Jews who collaborated with them—a tactic that would also be used by subsequent generations of what would become known as terrorists. Followers of other religions also resorted to methods that, today, might be termed as terrorism. One such group were the Assassins—an eleventh century offshoot of a Shia Muslim sect known as the Nizari Ismailis. Like the Sicarii, the Assassins were also given to stabbing their victims in broad daylight. The Assassins, whose name gave us the modern term, which literally meant 'hashish eater'—a reference to the ritualistic drug taking they were, perhaps falsely, rumoured to indulge in prior to undertaking missions—also used their action to send a message. Often, the Assassins' deeds were carried out at religious sites on holy days—a tactic to publicize their cause and incite others to do it.[9]

Sacrifice was the central element of the killings carried out by the Thugees—an Indian religious cult who ritually strangled their victims as an offering to the Hindu goddess of terror and destruction, Kali. In this case, the intent was to terrify the victim rather than influence any external audience. Between the seventh and the nineteenth centuries, the Thugees were responsible for as many as one million murders. Most probably, they were the last example of the religion-inspired terrorism until the phenomenon re-emerged some time ago.[10] In fact, before the nineteenth century, religion provided the only acceptable justification for terror. Secularized motivations for such actions did not emerge until the French Revolution.

The English word 'terrorism' is derived from the regime *de la terreur* that prevailed in France from 1793–1794. Originally an instrument of the state, the regime was designed to consolidate the power of the newly installed revolutionary government, protecting it from elements considered subversive. At that time terrorism was a positive term. The French revolutionary leader, Maximilien Robespierre, viewed it as vital if the new French Republic was to survive its infancy, proclaiming in 1794:

> Terror is nothing other than justice: prompt, severe, inflexible. It is, therefore, an emanation of virtue. It is not so much a special principle as it is a consequence of a general principle of democracy applied to our country's most urgent needs.

Under such justification, some 40,000 people were executed by the guillotine—a fate Robespierre and his top lieutenants would themselves suffer when, later the same year, his announcement of a new list of subversives led to a counter-inquisition by some in the revolutionary government who feared their names may be on the latest roll of 'traitors'. Before long, the Revolution devoured itself in an orgy of paranoiac bloodletting.[11]

Meanwhile, terrorism began to take on the negative connotations that it carries today. Initially, this was helped by the writings of people like the English political philosopher Edmund Burke who popularized the term 'terrorism' in English while demonizing its French revolutionary practitioners. The newly defined notions of nationalism and citizenship, which both caused and were the result of the French Revolution, also saw the emergence of a new predominantly secular terrorism. The appearance of political ideologies such as Marxism also created a fertile sense of unrest at the existing order, with terrorism offering a means for change. The Italian revolutionary Carlo Pisacane's theory of the 'propaganda of the deed', which recognized the utility of terrorism to deliver a message to an audience other than the target and draw attention and support to a cause, typified this new form of terrorism.[12]

The Narodnaya Volya (NV) was the one that first put Pisacane's thesis into practice. They were a Russian populist group that was formed in 1878 to oppose the Tsarist regime. The group's most famous deed, the assassination of Alexander II, also effectively sealed their fate by incurring the full wrath of the Tsarist regime. Unlike most other terrorist groups, the NV went to great lengths to avoid 'innocent' deaths, carefully choosing their targets, and often compromising operations rather than causing what would today be termed 'collateral damage'. The NV's actions inspired radicals elsewhere. Anarchist terrorist groups were particularly enamoured by the Russian populists. Nationalist groups such as those in Ireland and the Balkans adopted terrorism as a means to achieve their desired ends. As the nineteenth century gave way to the twentieth, terrorist attacks were carried out at such divergent places as India, Japan and the Ottoman Empire. Like Europe, terrorism arrived in the United States before the twentieth century. Not only were the anarchists active in the United States throughout the 1880s, the country's civil war had also witnessed acts deserving of the name and committed by both sides. The formation of the Ku Klux Klan also followed to fight the Reconstruction.[13]

State-sponsored terrorism had started to manifest itself long before the outbreak of the First World War in Europe. As an early indication, many officials in the Serbian government and military were reported to be involved in supporting, training and arming various Balkan groups that were active prior to the assassination of the Archduke Franz Ferdinand on 28 June 1914 in Sarajevo. The act was carried out by an activist of a group called the 'Young Bosnians' which is credited with setting in motion a chain of events leading to the war itself.[14]

Similarly, the Bulgarian government was responsible for the survival of the Macedonian Revolutionary Organization that was used against Yugoslavia as well as against domestic enemies. Political assassinations, deserving to be dubbed terrorism, dominated the 1930s. This led to proposals at the

League of Nations for conventions to prevent and punish terrorism as well as the establishment of an International Criminal Court. None of these proposals could materialize as they were overshadowed by events leading to the advent of the Second World War. In the inter-war years, state terrorism came to be associated with the oppressive measures taken by some totalitarian regimes, most notably in Nazi Germany, Fascist Italy and Stalinist Russia. More recently, governments, such as in Israel, have continually resorted to using the tool to subdue opposition, both within as well as beyond their territories.[15]

Bruce Hoffman argues that 'such usages are generally termed 'terror' in order to distinguish that phenomenon from 'terrorism' which is understood to be violence committed by non-state entities'.[16] However, not everyone agrees that terrorism should be considered a non-governmental undertaking. Jessica Sterns insists that, in deliberately bombarding civilians as a means of attacking enemy morale, states have indeed resorted to terrorism. Such instances not only include the Allied strategic bombing campaigns of the Second World War, but also the US dropping of the atomic bombs on Hiroshima and Nagasaki that ended the Pacific phase of the conflict.[17]

The involvement of non-state groups in terrorism that emerged in the wake of the Second World War is an open reality. The immediate focus of such activity shifted from Europe to that of the continent's various colonies. Spread across the Middle East, Asia and Africa, nascent nationalist movements resisted European attempts to resume colonial business after the defeat of the Axis powers. What triggered these indigenous movements was the recent quashing of the myth of European invincibility. Quite often, these nationalist and anti-colonial groups conducted guerrilla warfare that differed from terrorism as it tended towards larger bodies of 'irregulars' operating along more military lines than their terrorist counterparts. They also did so in the open from a defined geographical area over which they held sway. Such was the case in China and Indochina where such forces conducted insurgencies against the Kuomintang regime and the French colonial government respectively. Such campaigns were also fought in the rural and the urban areas by terrorist or guerrilla groups as against the French in Algeria.[18]

More such struggles were launched against the occupiers as in Kenya, Malaysia, Cyprus and Palestine that, by some critics, are construed as 'terrorist'. These groups quickly learned to exploit the burgeoning globalization of the world's media. As Hoffman puts it, 'They were the first to recognize the publicity value inherent in terrorism and to choreograph their violence for an audience far beyond the immediate geographical locations of their respective struggles'.[19] In the 1960s and 1970s, the number of these groups that may be described as 'terrorist' swelled to include not only nationalists, but those motivated by ethnic and ideological considerations. The former included groups such as the Basque ETA and the Provisional Irish Liberation Army while the latter comprised organizations such as the Red Army Faction and the Italian Red Brigades.[20]

Following the Second World War, Latin America saw the emergence of a number of guerrilla organizations, from the Shining Path in Peru to FARC in Colombia, who were driven by communist-socialist revolutionary causes and, as part of their guerrilla campaign, committed acts of terrorism. The successful communist revolution in Cuba had encouraged revolutionary guerrilla campaigns across the region. However, with the death of the charismatic guerrilla leader Che Guevara in 1967, the revolutionary guerrilla campaign in Latin America died down in the 1970s. During the 1980s, revolutionary and ethno-nationalist motives of non-state terrorism gave way to terrorism in the name of religion. The 1979 Iranian revolution, the anti-Soviet jihad in Afghanistan and the fall of the Soviet communist ideology are usually mentioned as the main reasons why religious terrorism came to dominate the end of the twentieth century and the beginning of the twenty-first century.

TERRORISM IN THE NAME OF RELIGION

Never before had religion become the principal source of terrorism at the global scale as it has since the beginning of the 1990s. The 11 September 2001 terrorist attacks against the United States allegedly carried out by those who deviated from the path of Islam and joined the al-Qaeda terror network under the misguided leadership of Osama bin Laden thus far represent the optimal stage of trans-national terrorism.

These and a number of other successive attacks against Muslim and Western targets claimed by al-Qaeda and other deviant religious outfits reflect the likely enormity of this form of terrorism in the twenty-first century.

Given the severity and volume of attacks carried out around the world by the deviant admirers or followers of Laden, the Western world seems to be preoccupied with Muslim fundamentalists or Islamist groups. We should not forget, however, that adherents of other religious traditions have been responsible for a significant number of terrorist attacks in recent years. In Israel, for instance, followers of the late Rabbi Meier Kahane were responsible for the execution of terrorist attacks or acts of 'vigilante justice' against Palestinians on the West Bank. These include the 1994 gun attack by Baruch Goldstein, a member of the right-wing Jewish group Kach, at the Al-Khalil Mosque in Hebron that killed thirty Muslim worshippers and injured dozens more. Extremists belonging to religions outside of the Abrahamic faiths have also practiced religious terrorism. In retaliation for what was perceived as desecration of the Golden Temple in Amritsar, the Sikhs resorted to assassinating the Indian Prime Minister Indira Gandhi that led to a wave of violence claiming more than 35,000 lives.[21]

While describing religious terrorism, most scholars tend to confuse the role of religion, depicting it as a goal rather than a means. In fact, terrorists are only using, or rather abusing, the name of religion. Their ultimate goal is essentially political and motivated solely by power ambitions. Given that, religious terrorism can be more logically and fairly defined as the deliberate use of organized violence against unarmed civilians for achieving political ends by using a bigoted religious creed as a means. The immediate purpose of a terrorist act, whether it is suicide bombing, targeted assassination or hijacking of an airliner, is to terrorize, intimidate and demobilize the general population. Among all other forms of terrorism such as ethno-nationalist and ideologically inspired terrorism, religious terrorism is the oldest, most consistent, and deadliest in terms of its current global reach and impact. Religious terrorists can hail from either the main religious faiths or small religious cults, and target not only the followers of other religious faiths, but also fellow believers refusing to follow their diktats.[22] At present, the operational scope of terrorism in the name of religion is no more limited to a particular country, or a specific region. Rather, it has become global, transcending international boundaries.[23]

According to Hoffman, the reason why religious terrorism results in so many more deaths than political terrorism 'may be found in the radically different value systems, mechanisms of legitimization and justification, concepts of morality, and worldviews embraced by the religious terrorist'.[24]

'Holy terror' contains a value system that stands in opposition to 'secular terror'. Secular terrorists operate within the realm of a dominant political and cultural framework. They want to win, to defeat the political system oppressing them. Their goal may be to destroy social structure, but they want to put something in its place. Secular terrorists would rather make allies than discriminately kill their enemies. Holy terrorists, however, are under no such constraints. They see the world as a battlefield between the forces of light and darkness. Winning is not described in political terms. The enemy must be totally destroyed. For political terrorists, killing is the outcome of an operation. Again, religious terrorists differ. Holy terrorists see killing as a 'sacramental act'.[25]

Religious terrorism afflicts every region of the world, developed and developing, Muslim and Western. However, it is most prevalent in the Middle East—the birthplace of Judaism, Christianity and Islam—and South and South-West Asia, the region historically known for a pacifist religious creed. In the Jewish state of Israel, terrorist organizations such as Kach and Kahane Chai aim to establish a Greater Israel of biblical times. For the purpose, they have committed several acts of terrorism against innocent Palestinians. The state of Israel, also, has itself been involved in some of the most gruesome acts of terrorism in contemporary times. As for Palestinians, there are individuals and entities among them or outside of them who have deviated from the path of true Islam and adopted violence in order to pursue their largely pragmatic political agendas. This has not only created friction among Palestinians who are peacefully struggling against heavy odds, but also tarnished the image of Islam.

As for South and South-West Asia, both Afghanistan and Pakistan have suffered the most from terrorism committed by the Taliban and al-Qaeda, who constitute the most prominent groups that have deviated from the path of their true faith by adopting a violent course that negates the spirit of jihad in its truest sense. But terrorism in this region undertaken in the name of religion is not restricted to the Taliban or al-Qaeda alone. Other examples include the conflict between the separatist Tamil-speaking Hindus and the ruling Sinhalese-speaking Buddhists in Sri Lanka, and the Hindu extremist violence against the minority Muslim, Christian and Sikh populace in India.[26] In the 1980s, the Sikhs also invoked their faith to commit terrorism in the East Punjab state of India, a terrorist wave that led to the assassination of former Indian Prime Minister Indira Gandhi.

In South-East Asia, religiously deviant organizations such as Abu Sayyaf in the Philippines and Malaysia and Jemaah Islamiyah in Indonesia have been involved in a number of terrorist acts targeting Western tourists, the most recent and lethal being the alleged bombing in Bali in November 2002 by militants of Jemaah Islamiyah.

Africa is not far behind in the contemporary wave of religious terrorism. In Algeria, the deviant religious entities such as the Armed Islamic Group do not spare the ruling regime or the general public in their terrorist operations. Nigeria and Kenya are two other African states depicting a growing trend of indigenous or trans-national religious terrorism. In the Balkan wars of the 1990s, Catholic Croats fought with Orthodox Serbs, and Orthodox Serbs fought against the Muslims of Bosnia and Kosovo. Each side accused the other of practicing terrorism. In Kosovo, for example, while the terrorism committed by Serbian forces of the Yugoslav federation was quite obvious, the Serb leadership accused the Kosovo Liberation Army of committing terrorism. When NATO started to bomb Yugoslavia, the Slavic-Orthodox Serb leadership even perceived a Western Christian conspiracy in it.[27]

In the Eastern Mediterranean island of Cyprus, the Muslim Turks have been at the receiving end of Greek Orthodox Christianity's Hellenic ambition of Enosis, the island's unification with Greece. In Eurasia, the two conflict situations—the dispute over Nagorno-Karabakh between Azerbaijan and Armenia, and the Chechen independence movement in the Russian federation—involve much of the same ethno-religious tendency, except that the issue of Chechnya is believed to be closely associated with al-Qaeda. In Central Asia, deviant religious groups like the Islamic Movement of Uzbekistan have committed a number of terrorist attacks against foreigners and government authorities in Uzbekistan and Kyrgyzstan.[28]

Religious terrorism also exists in the Western or developed world, though on a smaller scale than in the developing or Muslim parts of the world. In Northern Ireland, for instance, religion has fuelled the passions of the rival Protestant and Catholic extremists. Catholic extremists use the Catholic label to describe nationalistic revolutionaries who want no part of Britain. Protestant extremists use the Protestant label to define who will use terrorism to keep Northern Ireland associated with the United Kingdom. That explains why the

Catholic Sinn Fein and Protestant Ulster Unionists disagree over the power sharing formula in Northern Ireland and demilitarization of the Irish Republican Army.[29]

Terrorism by doomsday or apocalyptic religious cults has affected in particular Japan and the United States. Apocalyptic cults believe that the world is coming to an end and that members of the cult will play some role in the eschatological event. Doomsday cults believe they must take offensive action to bring about the end of the world. In March 1995, the Aum Shinrikyo (Supreme Truth) Sarin gas attack on Tokyo's subways killed twelve and injured more than 5,000. It was the world's first mass-scale chemical terrorist attack. The 1993 debacle in Waco, Texas, where seventy-four persons were killed, including twenty-one children, and the eighty-one-day standoff between the Freemen, a Montana militia organization, and the FBI in April 1996, which concluded peacefully, are two recent examples of the growth of religious cults and their terrorist implications in the United States. Religious extremist movements in the United States, in addition to such apocalyptic cults, include Black supremacy groups such as the Nation of Yahweh, white supremacists like the Ku Klux Klan and other Christian identity movements like the Aryan Nations.[30]

It is our misfortune that terrorism exercised by groups subscribing to a deviant creed in the world of Islam has become widespread in the past couple of decades. They have targeted Saudi Arabia and other Muslim nations as much as they have targeted the Western countries. The 11 September

2001 terrorist attacks against the United States and a number of terrorist attacks against other countries prove that religious terrorism in the twenty-first century will involve an enemy who is invisible and unpredictable, who acts without a stated military objective, does not spare even a power with the most awesome military capability, and aims at mass killing.[31] Fighting such an enemy requires new and multi-pronged approaches, employing military, political and economic means. However, de-radicalizing terrorist networks like al-Qaeda is an uphill task, which may not be accomplished as long as the larger context in which deviant religious culture flourishes is properly understood.

John Esposito writes:

Like all the world's major religious traditions, Islam has its extremist fringe. Osama bin Laden's steady dose of proclamations and threats has assumed that Islam, not just extremism or terrorism, receives special treatment. The climate today is one in which questions can be asked and statements can be made about Islam, not simply about the beliefs and actions of extremists, that would not be tolerated if directed at Judaism and Christianity. The danger of this approach is to overlook the fact that militant jihad movements and terrorism are not just the products of warped individuals and religious doctrines, whether mainstream or extremist interpretations, but of political and economic conditions.[32]

Given that, it may be a mistake to equate Islam with terrorism. In fact, the meaning of 'greater jihad' in Islam is the struggle for non-violent, positivist and selfless pursuits in the life of a Muslim. Even jihad's military usage is meant to be for defensive purposes. This is not to say that deviant religious figures within the world of Islam have never invoked jihad to justify their killing of Muslims and non-Muslims in history. They have, and continue to until this day. However, what we need to understand is that the doctrine of jihad is not the product of a single authoritative individual or organization's interpretation. Rather, it is the product of diverse individuals and authorities interpreting and applying the principles of sacred texts in specific historical and political contexts.[33] It is, therefore, important to place the issue of terrorism in the real Islamic perspective.

NOTES

1. Weinberg, op. cit., pp. 4–5.
2. Ibid.
3. Ibid., pp. 6–8.
4. Ibid.
5. Louise Richardson, *Terrorists: Understanding the Enemy, Containing the Threat* (New York: Random House, 2006), p. 20.
6. Paul R. Pillar, *Terrorism and US Foreign Policy* (Washington, DC: Brookings Institute Press, 2001), p. vii.
7. Reich, op. cit.
8. Samuel P. Huntington, *The Clash of Civilizations and the Remaking of World Order* (New York: Simon & Schuster, 1996), pp. 45–46.
9. Hoffman, op. cit., pp. 87–92.
10. Ibid.
11. Weinberg, op. cit., pp. 2–3.
12. Hoffman, op. cit., p. 17.

13. Jessica Stern, *The Ultimate Terrorists* (Cambridge: Harvard University Press, 2001), pp. 16–17.

14. Hoffman, op. cit., pp. 20–23.

15. Weinberg, op. cit., p. 26.

16. Ibid., p. 25.

17. Stern, p. 14.

18. Weinberg, op. cit., pp. 29–30.

19. Ibid., p. 65.

20. Ibid., pp. 34–35.

21. Ishtiaq Ahmad, 'Religious Terrorism,' in Palmer Fernandez, ed., *Encyclopaedia of Religion and War* (New York: Berkshire/Routledge, 2003), pp. 421–28.

22. Ibid.

23. Ahmad, 'Simplifying a Complex Issue,' op. cit.

24. See Hoffman, op. cit., pp. 87–92 and Stern, op. cit., pp. 1–10.

25. John White, *Terrorism: An Introduction* (Belmont, CA: Wadsworth, 2002), p. 51.

26. William Maley, *Fundamentalism Reborn: Afghanistan and the Taliban* (London: C. Hurst and Co., 1998).

27. Ibid.

28. Ibid.

29. Ahmad, op. cit.

30. Hoffman, op. cit., pp. 105–127.

31. Strobe Talbott and Nayan Chanda, *The Age of Terror: America and the World after September 11* (New York: Basic Books, 2001); and Walter Laqueur, *The New Terrorism* (New York: Oxford University Press, 1999), p. 5.

32. John Esposito, *Unholy War: Terror in the Name of Islam* (New York: Oxford University Press, 2002), p. 152.

33. Ahmad, 'Simplifying a Complex Issue,' op. cit.

3

The Islamic Perspective on Terrorism

O, Mankind, we have created you from male and female and made you into nations and tribes that you may know one another. Verily, the most honourable of you before God is the one who is most pious.[1]

This eternal call from Almighty God represents the true spirit of Islam, a religion of peace, love, tolerance, and brotherhood relevant for all ages and the entire humanity. Islam does not advocate or condone terrorism. The term 'terrorism' is not mentioned in the holy Qur'an literally, but it is expressed in other words such as mischief in the land, trespass, war or injustice. A careful examination of the holy Qur'an reveals deep concern about the security of souls, money, and honour. Accordingly, the holy Qur'an emphatically decries deeds that spoil these benefits (blessings) for the common people.

The overwhelming theme of the holy Qur'an is peace, as long as there is no oppression or injustice. According to the holy Qur'an, relations of Muslims with non-Muslims are strictly based on peace, confidence, tolerance and respect for each other. Islam forbids the killing of innocent people irrespective of their religions or beliefs. The holy Qur'an clearly commands: 'There shall be no compulsion in religion',[2] instructing the holy Prophet Muhammad (PBUH) not to force people to convert to Islam, unless they wish to do so by their own conviction. This reflects the tolerance of Islam. After all, the essence of almost all religions, including Islam, is peace, tolerance, love, freedom of beliefs and mutual understanding.

While Islam clearly calls upon all Muslims to defend themselves, it simultaneously obliges them not to be the aggressors. Islam is also very clear about the conduct of Muslims in war and in peace. Kindness and tolerance are the main teachings for Muslims in both situations. Muslim fighters are not allowed to harm a child, a woman or the elderly during a military campaign. They are not even permitted to cut down a tree in an enemy's land. The Qur'an emphasizes that 'killing one person without justice is as if killing the whole of humanity, and saving one person is as if saving the entire humanity'.[3] How then could a religion such as Islam condone terrorism?

ISLAM FORBIDS TERRORISM

Terrorism is to kill or harm innocent people. This is a direct contradiction of the teachings of Islam that dictate the opposite. In fact, the kindness of Islam is extended even to animals. A man was promised Paradise for providing a thirsty dog with water while a woman was promised hell for denying her cat any food (*Hadith*). How could anyone then assume that Islam is capable of terrorism? However, misinterpretation of Islamic teachings and the adoption of extremist positions of intolerance have been, and continue to be, used as the ideological foundation for various terrorist groups which are misusing the name of Islam to commit acts of terrorism. Al-Qaeda is, no doubt, a leading name among such groups, but religious misinterpretations, extremism and intolerance have been used as the basis for terrorist ideological beliefs and actions by other religious groups as well.[4]

Islam has recommended severe punishment for those who kill or commit mischief throughout the land. Terrorists fall in this category.[5] This indicates clearly the lawful punishment of those who wage war, and strive to spread mischief. Here we are not highlighting the details of waging war or punishment as explained by jurists, but two important points need to be discussed.

First, waging war is a crime that has a great impact upon national security. It causes panic and fear among the people. Muslim rulers (guardians) are responsible for preserving security that is part of the broader public interest. Secondly, application of this punishment contributes greatly to preserving security. On the other hand, negligence of this punishment, together with other lawful punishments, would negatively affect security by increasing crimes in the society.[6]

Islam, like all world religions, neither supports nor requires the illegitimate use of violence or acts of terrorism. Islam does permit, and at times requires, Muslims to defend themselves, their families, their religion and their community from aggression. The earliest Qur'anic verses dealing with the right to engage in a defensive jihad, or struggle, were revealed shortly after the emigration of the holy Prophet Muhammad (PBUH) and his followers to Madinah in consequence of their persecution in Makkah. At a time when they were forced to fight for their lives, the holy Prophet Muhammad (PBUH) is told: 'Leave is given to those who fight because they were wronged—surely God is able to help them—who were expelled from their homes wrongfully for saying, "Our Lord is God".'[7] The defensive nature of jihad is clearly emphasized in the holy Qur'an: 'And fight in the way of God with those who fight you, but aggress not: God loves not the aggressors'.[8]

The holy Qur'an also provides detailed guidelines and regulations regarding the conduct of wars: who is to fight and who is exempted,[9] when hostilities must cease[10] and how prisoners should be treated.[11] Most importantly, the holy Qur'an emphasizes that the response to violence and aggression must be proportionate.[12] However, Qur'anic verses also underscore that peace, not violence and warfare, is the norm. Permission to fight the enemy is balanced by a strong mandate for making peace: 'If your enemy inclines toward peace, then you, too, should seek peace and put your trust in God',[13] and 'Had God wished, He would have made them dominate you, and so, if they leave you alone and do not fight you and offer you peace, then God allows you no way against them'.[14] Islam forbids the killing of non-combatants.

But what of those verses, sometimes referred to as the 'sword verses', that call for killing unbelievers, such as 'When the sacred months have passed, slay the idolaters wherever you find them, and take them, and confine them, and lie in wait for them at every place of ambush'?[15] This is one of a number of Qur'anic verses that are selectively cited to demonstrate the supposedly violent nature of Islam and its scripture. In fact, however, the passage above is followed and qualified by, 'But if they repent and fulfil their devotional obligations and pay the *Zakat* (charity), then let them go their way, for God is forgiving and kind'.[16] The same is true of another often quoted verse: 'Fight those who believe not in God, Nor in the Last Day, Nor hold that forbidden which hath been forbidden by God and His Apostle, Nor hold the religion of truth (even if they are) of the People of the Book', which is often cited without the line that follows, 'until they pay the tax with willing submission, and feel themselves subdued'.[17]

In the perspective of Islamic Shariah, terrorism is a crime against humanity and warrants capital punishment. Spreading terror by way of random killing, injuring people, sabotaging public and private property and doing mischief in the land is a crime. The holy Qur'an says:

> The recompense of those who wage war against Allah and His Messenger and make mischief in the land is only that they shall be killed or crucified, or their hands and their feet be cut off from opposite sides, or they be exiled from the land. That is their disgrace in this world, and a great torment is theirs in the Hereafter.[18]

The offenders should be fought only until they cease hostilities toward Muslims, implying that those not initiating hostilities cannot be targeted. And last, if an enemy requests peace, it must be given: 'And if they incline to peace, then incline to it and trust in Allah; surely He is the Hearing, the Knowing'.

The holy Qur'an continues:

And when he turns away (from you O' Muhammad, [PBUH]), his effort in the land is to make mischief therein and to destroy the crops and the cattle, and Allah likes not mischief.[19]

But seek, with that (wealth) which Allah has bestowed on you, the home of the Hereafter, and forget not your portion of lawful enjoyment in this world; and do good as Allah has been good to you, and seek not mischief in the land. Verily, Allah likes not the *Mufsidun* (those who commit great crimes and sins, oppressors, tyrants, mischief-makers, corruptors).[20]

And whoever kills a believer intentionally, his recompense is Hell to abide therein; and the wrath and the curse of Allah are upon him, and a great punishment is prepared for him.[21]

THE REAL MEANING OF JIHAD

In Islam, Jihad means the internal and external human struggle to follow the right and the just path of Almighty God. This struggle manifests itself both internally and externally. Internal jihad is jihad within oneself to be a better person, to resist human temptations and eradicate character flaws such as greed. This is the greater jihad. The second, external form of jihad is personal conduct at a time of war or conflict. The holy Prophet (PBUH) is said to have remarked when he came home from a battle: 'We return from the lesser jihad to the greater jihad'. This shows the importance of the constant internal struggle that we all face within ourselves. It is the non-violent struggle that makes us become better people. The greater, internal jihad is seen as more important than the lesser, external jihad.

In particular, the Qur'anic reference to jihad has fallen to such misuse and misinterpretation. Muslim jurists classify 'jihad' into four different categories:[22]

1. Jihad means intense effort of the heart, which represents the internal spiritual and moral struggle and aims at victory over the ego;
2. Jihad means intense effort of the tongue, which represents calm preaching and teaching of the morals of Islam;
3. Jihad means intense effort of the hand, which represents the setting forth of good conduct as an example for the Islamic community and others; and
4. Jihad means intense effort of the sword, which corresponds to conflict with the enemies of the Islamic community in circumstances where believers are persecuted and their freedom curtailed.

Jihad of the sword is further sub-divided into six categories that are regulated by certain conditions to minimize violence and damage done to people and property.[23] These include:

1. Jihad against the enemies of God;
2. Jihad for the defence of frontiers;
3. Jihad against apostates;
4. Jihad against secessionists;
5. Jihad against groups that disturb public security, and
6. Jihad against monotheists who refuse to pay the capitation tax.

There is, however, general consensus among Muslim jurists that jihad of the sword represents a concerted effort to overcome the evil found in human society so that peace and justice is achieved for the entire global humanity and not just for the Muslims alone. It is a humanitarian goal to which all Muslims are obliged to be fully committed. If terrorism is an evil, then it has to be fought with the jihad of the sword if all other forms of jihad have been fully utilized. And in this struggle, the Muslims are required under Islam to engage in a concerted cooperative effort with the non-Muslims, since the implications of terrorism for both are equally grave.

ISLAMIC TRADITION OF PEACEFUL CO-EXISTENCE

While the world religions have piles of records of glorious achievements, there are also examples of the misuse of religion to accomplish selfish goals or distorted objectives. However, the historical religions have shown exemplary resilience to such misuses by re-emerging from these stark periods through the efforts of the faithful. When the noble ideals of Islam are breached, it is, in fact, a breach and betrayal of the tradition that is sacred to its followers. Therefore, such movements, despite their claims, should not be confused with the enduring historical legacy of Islam. There is no reason why religion should become a pretext for fuelling conflict, hatred and violence. On the contrary, religious sentiment should be the principal antidote to violence and division. In the current perspective, there is a dire need for individuals and religious communities to clearly manifest a complete rejection of violence. There is no religious end that can justify the practice of a man committing violence against another man.

Islam believes in diversity of religions. It actually took birth in the context of Judaism and Christianity being the prevailing religions of the time. Islam shows a special respect towards Judaism and Christianity because of the common faith heritage. Islam expects the followers of these religions to live an upright life as the wish of the Creator. The practical manifestation of Islam's conduct *vis-à-vis* the Jews and Christians, the other two peoples of the holy books and adherents of Abrahamic religions, is clear from the way the Muslim rulers and people dealt with them throughout the Golden Age of Muslims, which started in the eighth century and continued for several centuries. In Baghdad under the Abbasids and in Andalusia under successive Muslim rulers,

Christians and Jews not only shared unprecedented levels of prosperity with fellow Muslims, but they also equally contributed to the growth of Islamic scientific and artistic revolution characterizing the Golden Age of Islam.

This happened because the holy Qur'an commands Muslims to be extremely tolerant of their Jewish and Christian counterparts in religion. The holy Qur'an teaches: 'And those who follow the Jewish (scriptures), and the Christians and the Sabians—and who believe in Allah and the Last Day, and work righteousness, shall have their reward with their Lord'.[24] The holy Prophet Muhammad (PBUH) gave priority to seeking reconciliation and peace with Christians and Jews as well as with other opponents and enemies. The holy Qur'an strictly forbid the committing of any terrorist activity that may endanger peoples' lives, be they Muslim or non-Muslim. These crimes are described in the holy Qur'an as 'the Great Sin'.

In the West, Muslims are frequently labelled as terrorists and killers, and Islam is portrayed as a religion that incites violence and hatred. The fact is that Muslims, as a whole, do not believe in terrorism, and Islam abhors violence in any form and shape. It is, however, true that there are groups of people who call themselves Muslims, but have deviated from the path of Islam. It is they who commit acts of terrorism. It is important to note that while committing terrorism, such deviant individuals or groups do not make any distinction between Muslims and non-Muslims. It is this deviant category of people in the world of Islam whose deeds and behaviour contradict how Muslims are religiously obliged to conduct themselves in life under the principles of Islam.

It is also important to note that this problem, i.e. the gap between what religion says and how some of its followers behave, is not peculiar to Islam. Judaism, Christianity, Hinduism, in fact all of the world's religions or religious cults, have shown such deviant tendencies and their militaristic outcomes. The followers of many religions often focus on what is different, i.e. theological aspects and rituals, instead of focusing on what is common, i.e. values and principles. From such an approach stem the differences, which are fed upon ambitions and narrow interests. Consequently, hatred, conflict, violence, war and prejudice become the outcome of such an approach.

Karen Armstrong, the world-renowned scholar of comparative religions, describes the Qur'an as the most pluralist scripture, as it recognizes all the prophets that came before Prophet Muhammad (PBUH). Given that, Islam has a lot to offer to the people of other religious traditions, especially Judaism and Christianity. They need to understand that the real spirit of Islam revolves around the idea of compassion:

In Islam, Muslims have looked for God in history. Their sacred scripture, the Qur'an, gave them a historical mission. Their chief duty was to create a just community in which all members, even the most weak and vulnerable, were treated with absolute respect. The experience of building such a society and living in it would give them intimations of the divine, because they would be living in accordance with God's will.[25]

The Qur'an, Karen argues,

> forbids aggressive warfare and permits war only in self-defence. The moment the enemy sues for peace, the Qur'an insists that Muslims must lay down their arms and accept whatever terms are offered, even if they are disadvantageous. Later, *Shariah* forbade Muslims to attack a country where Muslims were permitted to practice their faith freely; the killing of civilians was prohibited, as were the destruction of property and the use of fire in warfare.[26]

Islam, as was revealed in the Qur'an, has advocated tolerance and moderation. Islam never promoted violence or hatred. Islam looks forward towards the future, not backwards to the past. Islam focuses upon promoting its own principles, not being detracted by concepts or ideas of others. The Qur'an sometimes narrates differences between nations and their behaviour, but most of the time focuses on what is common, i.e. Unity of Mankind, Unity of Religion and Oneness of God. Even when it refers to differences between nations and religious practices, the Qur'an calls for respect for all deities even if we believe they are false ones.

'Don't insult the deities of the non-believers in Allah so as not to incite them to insult Allah'.[27] Islam obliges Muslims to respect the adherents of all other faiths, and respect what they worship. There is only one path that the Qur'an recommends for Muslims, and this is the path of peace and reconciliation. Almighty Allah has shown us that dialogue is the way to bridge gaps and to narrow down differences. Suffice to recall the ceremony of Hijat Al Wadaie (the last pilgrimage of Prophet Muhammad [PBUH]), or even the history of the five pious caliphs and how they conducted the affairs of the Muslim nation of their time.

Remember also the glory of the Islamic civilization during the Golden Age of Islam. That became a reality when the Muslims decided to make a difference in this world. They acquired all possible knowledge from other civilizations of the day: the Greeks, the Chinese, the Indians, and made their own mark on this knowledge. They advanced themselves in science and technology, art and literature, and reached the apex of modernity—a glorious period that continued for centuries. It is exactly this spirit of learning that the Muslims need today, and need urgently. There is no way out of the Muslim debacle today except the one described by Almighty Allah in the Qur'an: 'God will not change the situation in which a people are living unless they change themselves'.[28]

So, if one goes by the verdict of Almighty Allah, it is clearly in favour of a dialogue among civilizations, rather than a clash between civilizations. The world is no doubt lived by people of different races, ethnicities, and faiths. Islam stands for the recognition and appreciation of these differences, rather than making these differences a source of conflict. The Qur'an prefers oneness of humanity to its differential nature. While human civilization may have different ethno-religious contours, seen in its entirety, it is one human civilization. So, narrowing down differences is a principal religious obligation to bridge gaps within this single human civilization. The Qur'an refers to this common human destiny in the following words: 'We created you from male and female, we made you into tribes and nations to get acquainted and know each other'.[29]

As stated before, just as religious extremists in other faiths, including Judaism and Christianity, have misused their religions and misinterpreted their religious scriptures to justify acts of terrorism, some extremist organizations in the world of Islam, including al-Qaeda, have also misused the name of Islam and misinterpreted the word of the holy Qur'an to justify their acts of terrorism. It should be sufficiently clear from the preceding discussion that Islam forbids terrorism in the strongest terms and there are severe punishments prescribed for those who indulge in bringing harm to innocent human beings which is the primary motive of all acts of terrorism. Making any religion, least of all Islam, the basis for perpetrating crimes against fellow human beings is an abhorrent and heinous act that should be condemned by all people belonging to all religions and faiths.

NOTES

1. The holy Qur'an, Surah 49, Verse 1.
2. Ibid., Surah 2, Verse 256.
3. Ibid., Surah Al-Maida, Verse 32.

4. Ishtiaq Ahmad, 'Why Islam Forbids Terrorism,' *Weekly Pulse*, 28 June–3 July 2008.

5. The holy Qur'an, Surah 5, Verses 33–34.

6. Ibid., Surah 5, Verse 11.

7. Ibid., Surah 22, Verse 39.

8. Ibid., Surah 2, Verse 190.

9. Ibid., Surah 48, Verse 17; Surah 9, Verse 91.

10. Ibid., Surah 2, Verse 192.

11. Ibid., Surah 47, Verse 4.

12. Ibid., Surah 2, Verse 294.

13. Ibid., Surah 8, Verse 61.

14. Ibid., Surah 4, Verse 90.

15. Ibid., Surah 9, Verse 5.

16. Ibid., Surah 9, Verse 5.

17. Ibid., Surah 9, Verse 29.

18. Ibid., Surah 5, Verse 33.

19. Ibid., Surah 2, Verse 205.

20. Ibid., Surah 28, Verse 77.

21. Ibid., Surah 4, Verse 93.

22. Marcel A. Boisard, *Jihad: A Commitment to Universal Peace* (Indianapolis: American Trust Publication 1988), pp. 24–25.

23. Ibid.

24. The holy Qur'an, Surah 2, Verse 148; Surah 22, Verse 67.

25. Ishtiaq Ahmad, 'Karen Armstrong on Islamic Legacy of Compassion,' *Weekly Pulse*, 8–14 February 2008.

26. Ibid.

27. The holy Qur'an, Surah Al-An'am, Verse 108.

28. Ibid., Surah Al-Ra'd, Verse 11.

29. Ibid., Surah Al-Hujurat, Verse 13.

4

Root Causes of Terrorism

Almost all the leading works on terrorism, including those emanating from Western academia and policy think tanks, underscore the significance of addressing the root causes of terrorism as a means for effectively combating terrorism. The problem arises when they attempt to identify the root causes. For instance, Bruce Hoffman, the author of the 1998 book *Inside Terrorism*,[1] is a known Western authority on religious terrorism. However, his discourse on religious terrorism is consistently marked by a major distortion, whereby religion is presented as a goal rather than as a means—which is actually the case—when it comes to analysing the root causes of the al-Qaeda-led international terrorist wave of the 1990s and beyond. Huntington had also put religion at the core of his 'clash of civilizations' thesis pertaining to the relationship between 'Islam and the West' in the contemporary era. However, in the immediate aftermath of the terrorist events of 11 September 2001 in the United States, he was compelled to revise it by arguing, in a *Newsweek* article titled 'The Age of Muslim Wars',[2] that the root causes of international terrorism occurring in the name of Islam are essentially political, including, among others, the unresolved conflicts of the Muslim world such as Palestine and the Muslim perceptions of the US practicing a policy of 'double-standards' towards these conflicts.

Before discussing how the world is responding to international terrorism, especially what strategies Saudi Arabia and other Muslim countries have adopted against domestic and international terrorism, it is important to pinpoint what the actual root causes of terrorism are. No counter-terrorism strategy, whether already operational or still in the conceptual stage, can ever succeed if it is not grounded in the due understanding of the root causes of terrorism, especially their relative potential for generating extremism and terrorism.

PROBLEM WITH GENERALIZATIONS

In so far as the root causes of terrorism, or the conditions that give rise to it, are concerned, the generalized explanations tend to identify poverty, the lack of democracy or history as prominent factors causing terrorist violence. However, a closer look at the ground reality reveals that this is not always the case. Africa is mostly poverty ridden and politically authoritarian and the Western world is rich and democratic, yet the latter has seen more terrorism than the former. As for historical justification, South Asia had not seen any terrorist campaign until the 1970s. Since then, the region has been gripped by an unending wave of terrorist violence. In the 1950s and 1960s, terrorism was more visible in Latin America in the wake of the communist-socialist revolutionary guerrilla struggles, and parts of Asia and Africa were undergoing anti-colonial ethno-nationalist struggles. Now it is no more the case. The Middle East, on the other hand, has seen somewhat a consistent pattern of non-state terrorist violence. So, it depends from situation-to-situation, and time-to-time, which country or which region comes under terrorist threat. The root causes of terrorism, therefore, have to be issue-, situation- and time-specific.

But then, again, we cannot ignore poverty as an important root cause of terrorism. Take, for instance, the case of the *madrassa*. Most authors, while rejecting the argument that some individuals are born terrorists, or that something is inherently wrong with their mental state, point out that an important cause of terrorism is the sort of learning process that students enrolled in *madrassa*s undergo. The students are brainwashed through consistent exposure to 'hate literature', and the end product is a robot-like person ready to undertake any act, including that of suicide bombing. First of all, such arguments cannot be generalized to the extent of castigating the entire *madrassa* culture in Islamic history, which, in fact, laid the basis of higher learning in Europe and the consequent Western renaissance. Even if the above argument has some rational basis in the case of a handful of *madrassa*s generating extremism and terrorism by deviant individuals and organizations, the story will still be incomplete if the emphasis remains only on the *madrassa* environment. It is only the children of the poor, for whom the state fails to provide educational facilities, or who cannot afford to educate their children in normal schools, who get enrolled in these *madrassa*s which are philanthropist institutions based on funding by Islamic charities.

In retrospect, the heart of the matter is poverty, especially as regards instances of extremist and terrorist activities implicating some *madrassa*s. However, broadly speaking, for a large number of people in the world, the deprivation of the basic necessities of life, the lack of education and recourse to opportunities for ensuring an honourable sustenance for themselves and their dependants is the fuel that ignites the fires of extremism and violence. There is a dire need for removing the gross inequities that exist in the world. Steps must be envisaged to ensure that all people of the world enjoy their inalienable rights and have free access to opportunities to progress in life without any discrimination on the basis of faith, class, colour or creed.[3]

DIVERSITY OF REASONS

The reasons behind terrorism are as diverse as the types of people who commit terrorist attacks. Terrorists often believe that they have exhausted all attempts for legitimate religious or political change and have no other option to bring recognition for their cause and change in the society they live in. However, terrorists intentionally target civilians in order to gain publicity. Political oppression, religious intolerance and divine revelation are a few of the most common reasons cited by terrorists as justification for their attacks. Political injustice and resistance to military occupation are, perhaps, the most often cited causes behind terrorism. Terrorists often agree that the opposing government has not responded to legitimate demands for political change and, consequently, they must take up arms. The terrorists will often justify their criminal attacks on unarmed civilians by arguing that the opposing military forces are too strong to oppose openly.[4]

Political and military action against governments that no longer respond to the needs of their populations is often justified. However, legitimate opposition to a government or military forces does not include attacks on unarmed civilians. Sometimes, citizens can achieve self-rule only by the use of revolutionary forces. Self-illusions of grandeur are common in the mentally disturbed, criminally insane and fanatical or religious terrorists. When illusions of grandeur and religious fanaticism affect small groups of people in leadership positions, it becomes easier to understand how heinous terrorist crimes are conceived and executed.[5]

Hate, prejudice and ignorance are the other factors motivating terrorists to carry out attacks upon unsuspecting civilians. These crimes are also motivated because of race, religious and sexual preferences. However, not all ethnic crimes are against individuals or property. In the largest domestic terrorist attack in United States history, Timothy McVeigh planned and executed the bombing of the Murrah building in Oklahoma City in 1995 that left 168 dead and hundreds wounded. McVeigh believed that the United States government no longer represented the majority of its citizens and hoped to spark a mass uprising with the attack and restore America to an all-white ethnic government. Ethnic cleansing in Bosnia and Herzegovina or the mass murders committed in Rwanda are other examples of ethnic terrorism. Single-issue terrorists believe so strongly in a cause that they feel compelled to act even individually to convince the world of their sincerity and do anything to bring recognition to their beliefs.[6]

Some terrorists use divine revelation as justification for racial, ethnic or religious terrorist attacks. Other terrorists attempt to spark a general uprising by a single strategically placed devastating attack designed to shatter the will of their enemies. Many terrorists argue that they are the victims of political and economic oppression and, because of the strength of the opposing state entities, they have no choice but to resort to bombings and random assaults.[7]

Terrorists have varying reasons or motives for their acts. Many politically motivated terrorists, whether of the left or the right, want to bring down an existing government or regime. Many religious terrorists want to attack those that they perceive as attacking their religion. Others want publicity for their cause. Suicide terrorists, almost always, have had one relative or close friend killed, maimed or abused by an enemy. There is also no single profile of terrorists. Most, but not all suicide terrorists, come from poor backgrounds, but some have university degrees. Most are male aged between 16 and 28 years, but 15 per cent are female and this percentage is rising.[8] Culture in general and religion in particular seem to be relatively unimportant in the phenomenon of terrorist suicide. Terrorist suicide, like any other suicide, is basically an individual rather than a group phenomenon: it is done by people who wish to die for personal reasons. The terrorist framework simply offers the excuse (rather than the real drive) for doing it and the legitimization for carrying it out in a violent manner.[9]

It is, therefore, amply clear that the reasons of terrorism are diverse and complicated. It may only be possible to delineate a set of reasons why individuals indulge in committing this heinous act, with or without the support of a group or organization. The origins encompass a multitude of social, cultural, political, religious, ethnic and economic factors. The one factor that is common to all acts of terrorism is that, whenever perpetrated, they cause untold suffering and misery among those who are targeted.

MUSLIM GRIEVANCES

In so far as the Muslim world is concerned, the root causes of terrorism are not difficult to trace. For centuries, the world of Islam has undergone subjugation at the hands of the West, in the run-up to European colonialism, during it, and even in its aftermath. Given that, it is but natural for reactionary tendencies to emerge in a section of the Muslim populace. Muslim immigrant communities in Western Europe or North America—whether of African, Arab or South Asian origin— have quite often confronted racism. But that is not the end of the story. In contemporary world history, most of the regional conflicts have seen Muslim communities being victimized by non-Muslim states. The Serbian atrocities against the Muslims of Bosnia and Kosovo, the cases of the Chechen and the Kashmiri Muslims, and above all, the Israeli state terror against Palestinians, who happen to be mostly Muslims, are major examples in this regard.

There is no justification for taking and preaching extreme positions, and no religion provides a basis for such attitudes. All religions preach tolerance and peaceful co-existence. Those few people who are engaged in a nefarious effort to promote the cult of extremism and violence are heretics and deviants. They must be controlled through a combined effort of all peace-loving nations of the world. It is, therefore, important to look into the causes of extremism and terrorism violence practiced by heretics and deviants in the name of Islam. Issues facing the Muslim world are political. Therefore, their root causes have to be political. Those practicing terrorism by citing these issues are also guided by political goals, and religion is only being used or abused as a means by them for justifying their terrorist activities. Any religious justification for terrorist activity is wrong, immoral and inhuman. And, as the discussion in the preceding chapter clearly manifests, terrorism in the name of Islam is not only un-Islamic, but also anti-Islam.

It is unfortunate that while the theory of religion preaches peace, its practice by a handful of deviants and heretics preaches violence. It is only by forging unity in their ranks that the Muslim people of the world can bridge this gap between theory that is subscribed to by a majority of them, and its practice that denotes only a tiny minority of miscreants. Terrorism is anti-Islam because intolerant and violent conduct *vis-à-vis* fellow Muslims and non-Muslims, especially the 'People of the Book', has never been a predominant tradition throughout Islamic history. It was essentially through a benevolent approach of love and peace and an effective campaign of winning the 'hearts and minds' that Muslims were able to make their mark on history in the West during the Dark Ages, extending their governance beyond the Arabian peninsula and the Middle East to regions as far away as Central Asia, South and South-East Asia, vast regions of the African continent, and even parts of Europe, including the Balkans and the Mediterranean.

What is, then, the problem now in an era that has seen organizations such as al-Qaeda and a number of its affiliates hijack the historically-tolerant and peaceful tradition of the Muslims in world affairs and, through their extremist words and terrorist practices, defame Muslims and the religion of Islam? There has to be some political context providing the fuel for their extremism and terrorism. Unresolved conflicts in the Muslim world, the duality of US/Western outlook *vis-à-vis* these conflicts, and recurrent instances of racism as part of the growing wave of Islamophobia in the Western world constitute the current global political context which is used by deviant organizations such as al-Qaeda to justify their extremism and terrorism.

In particular, there is a general perception in the Muslim world that the United States practices a policy of double standards when it comes to resolving disputes in the Muslim world. With regard to Palestine, the United States practices such a policy openly by supporting the state of Israel and ignoring Israel's suppression of Palestinian rights. The list of instances reflecting US duality *vis-à-vis* issues of Muslim suffering in history, and at present, is endless. Therefore, as long as the conflicts in the Muslim world, especially Palestine, exist, there will always be deviant individuals or groups in the world of Islam willing to practice terrorism using these conflicts as a justification and, in the process, abusing their religion. The unresolved conflicts provide the political context for their terrorist actions. In the absence of such context, they will have no justification for terrorist action.

THE PALESTINIAN PROBLEM

The Palestinian problem, above all, provides the most important political context for deviant organizations such as al-Qaeda to commit terrorism. However, by engaging in terrorist activities in the guise of fighting for Palestinian rights, such organizations not only further complicate the process of politically resolving the Palestinian issue, but also defame the religion of Islam. The Muslim world, by and large, stands shoulder to shoulder with the Palestinians in so far as the question of attaining their just and fair right to self-determination is concerned. This right can only be achieved if Israel vacates the Palestinian territories it occupied in 1967, agrees to repatriation of over three million Palestinian refugees to the land which once belonged to them, demolishes all the illegal Jewish settlements built on Palestinian lands, and accepts that East Jerusalem should be the capital of the new State of Palestine.

At present, the predominant view in the Muslim world on the Palestinian question is for a two-state solution, living side-by-side with complete security and stable peace. Exceptions in this regard are only a few state or non-state entities in the Middle East, who are pursuing a reactionary, militant course in an attempt to sabotage the broader Muslim world push towards an amicable Palestinian settlement. However, as long as Israel does not end its repressive policy against the Palestinians, and the United States and some of its Western allies continue to ignore the Israeli repression of Palestinians, no international or regional bid—whether by the Middle East Quartet or the Arab League—for solving the Palestinian problem will succeed. In the meantime, however, deviant entities will continue with their regressive agenda, thus further complicating a political settlement of the issue.

Israeli state terror against the Palestinians is expressed in manifold ways: through aerial bombardment of Palestinian homes, target killings of their leaders, checking the movement of Palestinians through hundreds of check-posts between the West Bank and Gaza, the siege of Gaza, building of the so-called 'security wall' around the West Bank, expanding illegal Jewish settlements in the West Bank, and continued blockade of Palestinian air, sea and land links with the outside world. The most blatant expression of Israeli state terrorism against the Palestinians was the recent Israeli air and ground assault on Gaza, which killed close to 1,500 innocent people, half of them women and children. The operation caused unprecedented devastation and, interestingly, ended with the accession to power of the US administration of President Barack Hussein Obama in January 2009.

The Israeli attack on Gaza received widespread international condemnation. The United Nation's General Assembly President Miguel D'Escoto Brockmann, UN Commissioner of Human Rights Navi Pillay, and UN Special Rapporteur for Human Rights in the Occupied Palestinian Territory Professor Richard Falk singled out Israel for committing the aggression, especially underlining the 'disproportionate' use of military force on the part of Israel. Professor Falk has said that Israeli air strikes on the Gaza Strip represent 'severe and massive violations of international humanitarian law as defined in the Geneva Conventions, both with regard to the obligations of an Occupying Power and in the requirements of the laws of war'. In his statement, Professor Falk said that Israel has committed multiple violations, which include collective punishment: the entire 1.5 million people who live in the crowded Gaza Strip are being punished for the illegal actions of a few militants. 'Israel is targeting civilians: the air strikes were aimed at civilian areas in one of the most crowded stretches of land in the world, certainly the most densely populated area of the Middle East. Israeli military action in the strip is "disproportionate", the air strikes have not only destroyed security compounds, but have killed and injured hundreds of civilians', Professor Falk said.[10]

Thus it is clear that it is not only the Muslim world that is concerned about the Palestinian plight at the hands of Israel. The condemnation of Israeli atrocities against Palestinians is truly global. South African leader and Nobel Peace Laureate Nelson Mandela and former US President Jimmy Carter have accused the state of Israel of practicing racism against the Palestinians. Back in 2001, Mandela had created a parallel between the Palestinian plight in the occupied territories and the situation confronting the majority black people of South Africa before the end of its white minority apartheid regime.

In a memo to *The New York Times'* columnist Thomas L. Friedman, published in March 2001,[11] Nelson Mandela had observed that the

> Palestinian–Israeli conflict is not just an issue of military occupation, and Israel is not a country that was established 'normally' and happened to occupy another country in 1967. Palestinians are not struggling for a 'state' but for freedom, liberation and equality, just like we were struggling for freedom in South Africa.

The problem of Palestine, Mandela argued, did not begin with the occupation of Palestinian territories by Israel in the 1967 war. It was rooted in the establishment of the state of Israel in 1948. That is why the issue of the return of millions of Palestinian refugees to the land of their origin was so crucial. He then argued that Israel was not thinking of a "state" (for Palestinians) but of "separation". The value of separation is measured in terms of the ability of Israel to keep the Jewish state Jewish, and not to have a Palestinian minority that could have the opportunity to become a majority at some time in the future. If this takes place, it would force Israel to either become a secular democratic or bi-national state, or to turn into a state of apartheid not only *de facto*, but also *de jure*.

According to Mandela,

apartheid is a crime against humanity. Israel has deprived millions of Palestinians of their liberty and property. It has perpetuated a system of gross racial discrimination and inequality. It has systematically incarcerated and tortured thousands of Palestinians, contrary to the rules of international law. It has, in particular, waged a war against a civilian population, in particular children.

In his 2007 book, *Palestine: Peace not Apartheid*, President Carter also equates the plight of today's Palestinians to the former victims of government-mandated racial separation in South Africa:

Israel is now following a system of apartheid, in which Israelis are dominant and Palestinians are deprived of basic human rights. Israel's continued control and colonization of Palestinian land have been the primary obstacles to a comprehensive peace agreement in the Holy Land.

According to Carter, UN Resolution 242 calls on Israel to return all territories occupied during the 1967 War and return to its pre-war borders. Until this happens, there will be no peace in Palestine.[12]

Palestinians have been denied their legitimate rights through inhuman policies followed by successive Israeli governments. The Palestinian people, like all other people of the world, have an inalienable right to their own country and it is denial of this basic right to them that is the principal cause of unrest in Palestine. As long as this right is denied to them, Palestine will continue to breed unrest. For resolution of the Palestinian problem, the comprehensive peace plan offered by King Abdullah bin Abdul Aziz provides a complete and rational basis. The plan, first published by Friedman in his *New York Times* column in February 2002,[13] and adopted by the Arab League Summit in March 2002, calls for 'full (Israeli) withdrawal from all occupied territories, in accord with the UN resolutions, including Jerusalem, for full normalization of relations (of Arab nations with Israel)'.

The Arab League Summit in Beirut, 27–28 March 2002, adopted the plan that was motivated by the resonance of the Palestinian plight in the Arab and Islamic community as well as by its desire for finalizing peace and ending the conflict. The summit declaration called for Israeli withdrawal from all territories occupied since 1967, the return of the Palestine refugees and establishment of a Palestinian state in the West Bank and Gaza Strip in exchange for Arab nations' recognition of Israel and normal relations. This was a major initiative for resolution of the Palestinian problem that has, over time, won widespread acknowledgement from not just the Muslim world, but also from the international community as a whole, except from the state of Israel, or its supporters in the United States. Instead of responding positively to the peace plan, Israelis have continued their repressive campaign in the occupied Palestinian territories.

THE WARS IN IRAQ AND AFGHANISTAN

Other Muslim world conflicts, such as Iraq and Afghanistan, provide the due political context for deviant groups to use them as a pretext for their terrorist activities. Consequently, the conflicts have only worsened and, in the process, helped defame the religion of Islam. In Iraq, al-Qaeda has been able to exploit the bloody sectarian strife accompanying the war that began with the US-led invasion of the country in March 2003. The terror network has succeeded in turning Iraq into a new suicide-bombing-ridden battlefield whose principal victims have been none other than Iraqi Muslims themselves. In Afghanistan, since the collapse of the Taliban regime in late 2001, the al-Qaeda-inspired and Taliban-led insurgency against NATO-led International Security Assistance Forces (ISAF) shows no sign of ending. The reasons for this have as much to do with NATO's inability to muster the required combat and financial support as with the failure of the post-Taliban Afghan government and its international partners to take credible initiatives regarding political governance, economic development and social progress in the war-torn country.

The wars in Iraq and Afghanistan have failed to address extremism and violence, creating immense unrest in the Muslim world. Having failed to address the menace of extremism and violence, these wars have, in fact, contributed to creating additional misgivings among the suffering people who generally give vent to their frustration by supporting the cause or fighting the forces that are waging these wars. This has contributed to broadening the scope of these conflicts and causing more bloodshed. Given that, there is a need for revisiting the logic behind the wars in Afghanistan and Iraq and engaging the combatants in a dialogue to find lasting solutions to the conflicts.[14]

The situation in Iraq may have relatively stabilized over time, but the war in Afghanistan continues to worsen. Again, as in the case of Palestine, we can only hope that the Obama administration, particularly its special representative for Afghanistan and Pakistan, Richard Holbrooke, the architect of the Dayton Accords which ended the Bosnian war, will make a difference in tackling the gigantic challenges that the war in Afghanistan poses to the Afghans, the nations in the region, and the wider world.

Iraq and Afghanistan are not the only examples where Western conduct has caused Muslim grievances, and fuelled extremism and terrorism by deviant organizations. In fact, we see a pattern in US–Western duality when it comes to other recent conflicts where Muslims have been at the receiving end. For example, European powers looked the other way when over eight thousand Bosnian Muslims were butchered by Serbian forces during the Balkan crisis of the 1990s. No one took notice of the killing of Muslims in Chechnya. Likewise, nobody in the West has ever addressed the human rights violations in Kashmir. In fact, in so far as Kashmir is concerned, it has been over half a century since the UN Security Council resolved to settle the issue through a plebiscite to determine the wishes of the Kashmiri people. While India and Pakistan have been engaged in a peace process since January 2004, and have implemented a number of Confidence-Building Measures (CBMs) to facilitate a Kashmiri settlement, in the absence of an early political settlement, the Kashmir issue may continue to provide the political context for deviant groups to engage in terrorist activities—just as it has been the case with other conflicts in the Muslim world such as Palestine, Iraq, and Afghanistan.

The November 2008 terror attacks in Mumbai jeopardized the peace process and brought the two countries close to war. If the international diplomacy, in which Saudi Arabia also played its part, had not prevailed, there was serious risk of the post-Mumbai crisis in the region to conflagrate. Given that, if and when the peace process between Pakistan and India resumes, the two countries, especially India, and the international community should seriously consider an urgent resolution of this over half a century old dispute. For, in the absence of such resolution, the unsettled Kashmir issue may continue to provide the political context for deviant groups to engage in terrorist activities—just as it has been the case with other Muslim world conflicts such as Palestine, Iraq and Afghanistan.

ISLAMOPHOBIA

The lingering conflicts in the Muslim world which provide the political context for terrorist actions are, no doubt, a major root cause of terrorism by deviant organizations. There is another, a more recent reason that has its roots in the history of Western orientalism and colonialism. Islamophobia is the latest expression of Western hostility towards the Muslim peoples. The predominant discourse in the European media at present reflects an increasing tide of animosity against Islam and Muslims living in Europe and America. For instance, a 2005 survey on Western perceptions of Islam and Muslims—which questioned more than 2,400 people in Britain, France, Germany, the Netherlands and the US—suggested that Muslims were rated lowest as compared to other religious groups. The survey noted that the portrayal of Arabs and Muslims was 'typically stereotypical and negative'. Nearly three-quarters of the respondents believed that the Western media depicted Arab Muslims and Islam accurately only half the time, not often.[15]

Various instances of racist victimization of Muslim immigrants in Europe, North America and Australia in the pre- and post-11 September 2001 period aside, the publication and republication of the blasphemous drawings of the holy Prophet Muhammad (PBUH) in Danish and other Western newspapers since September 2005, and the internet release of a film, '*Fitna*' by a Dutch lawmaker in March 2008 desecrating the verses of the holy Qur'an, have enraged the entire Muslim world populace. Some miscreants in the Western media and politics are, no doubt, engaged in an ill-intended campaign to hurt the religious sensitivities of Muslims by publishing blasphemous material and misreporting the words of the Islamic scripture, and inciting them for a militant-reactionary response.

Some deviant organizations have directly fallen into the trap set by these miscreants, and engaged in violent-terrorist acts. However, broadly speaking, the Muslim world's protest on the matter has been confined to public rallies and official reactions. Such recurrent instances of blasphemy, emanating especially from Denmark and the Netherlands, have, in fact, led to a global debate about the limits on freedom of expression, and the urgent need for balancing it with an obligatory respect for religion. Having said this, the fact remains that as long as some miscreants are bent upon defaming the religion of Islam and Muslims as a people, a viable political context will always be there for some deviants in the world to come up with a terrorist response to such blasphemous acts.

Whether it is the growing tide of Islamophobia in the Western world, or the continuingly unresolved conflicts in the Muslim world and Western duality towards them, they constitute the root causes of terrorism in the twenty-first century. Combating the international terrorist threat requires their urgent political resolution in a fair and equitable manner. While the responsibility to tackle Islamophobia and show fairness *vis-à-vis* conflicts in the Muslim world lies squarely on the shoulders of Western governments and societies, the Muslim states and societies are obliged to confront those who adopt terrorist tactics on issues which can only be settled politically. As for other root causes of terrorism such as poverty, while the context varies, these are issues afflicting the entire humanity, and therefore, they require a genuine universalistic solution.

NOTES

1. Hoffman, op. cit.
2. Samuel P. Huntington, 'The Age of Muslim Wars,' *Newsweek*, December 2001–January 2002.
3. See my interview: Sajjad Malik, 'Afghan, Iraq wars have fuelled terrorism, violence: Asseri,' *Daily Times*, 5 May 2008.
4. Carroll Payne, 'Reasons behind Terrorism', *Global Terrorism* (March 2002). Available from http://www.glopbalterrorism101.com/ ReasonsBehindTerrorism.html, accessed on 10 May 2008.
5. Ibid.
6. Ibid.
7. Ibid.
8. Harvey W. Kushner, 'Suicide Bombers: Business as Usual,' *Studies in Conflict and Terrorism*, Vol. 19 (1996), pp. 329–337.
9. A. Merari, 'The Readiness to Kill and Die: Suicidal Terrorism in the Middle East,' in W. Reich, ed., *Origins of Terrorism: Psychologies, Ideologies, Theologies and States of Mind* (New York: Cambridge University Press, 1998), p. 206.

10. As cited by Ishtiaq Ahmad, 'Palestinian Tragedy,' *Weekly Pulse*, 2–8 January 2009.

11. Thomas L. Friedman, 'Mandela Memo on Palestine, *The New York Times*, 28 March 2002.

12. Jimmy Carter, *Palestine: Peace not Apartheid* (New York: Simon & Schuster, 2007), pp. 125, 242.

13. Thomas L. Friedman, 'An Intriguing Signal from the Saudi Crown Prince,' *The New York Times*, 17 February 2002.

14. Malik, op. cit.

15. Ishtiaq Ahmad, 'West European Perceptions of Islam,' *Weekly Pulse*, 14–20 April 2006.

5

Saudi Strategy against Terrorism:
Domestic Dimensions

> I vow to my fellow citizens, and to the friends who reside among us, that the State will be vigilant about their security and well being. Our nation is capable, by the Grace of God Almighty and the unity of its citizens, to confront and destroy the threat posed by a deviant few and those who endorse or support them. With the help of God Almighty, we shall prevail.[1]

That was how King Abdullah bin Abdul Aziz (then Crown Prince) had responded to three suicide bombings of housing compounds in Riyadh on 13 May 2003, which claimed thirty-four innocent lives. This was not the first terrorist attack against the Saudi people. In the past few decades, the Kingdom has faced terrorism several times. In each instance, terrorists may have caused irreparable damage to life and property, but the Saudi resolve to combat terrorism has only grown in intensity and scope.

In 1979, a group of extremists had seized the Grand Holy Mosque at Makkah. However, after intense fighting, the government was able to regain control and the surviving terrorists were brought to justice.[2] In the 1990s, there were several terrorist bombings, including the 1995 terrorist act in

Riyadh, and the 1996 terrorist bombing in Khobar. The May 2003 terrorist incident was followed by another terrorist bombing in Almohiya housing compound in Riyadh on 10 November 2003, which claimed seventeen innocent lives.[3]

Since Saudi Arabia has faced terrorism for decades, its counter-terrorism efforts, including domestic measures and international initiatives, are also decades old. However, given the intensity of terrorist activity against the Kingdom since the 11 September 2001 attacks in the United States, the Saudi authorities have become more proactive in combating terrorism at the national and international level. But the fact remains that the Saudi fight against terrorism predates 11 September 2001. It was, therefore, quite unfortunate that, in the aftermath of the terrorist attacks in the United States, the Kingdom of Saudi Arabia came under the spotlight merely because a majority of the perpetrators happened to be Saudi citizens. In the United States in particular, and the Western world in general, a considerable amount of insinuating literature proliferated casting aspersions on the Kingdom, its leadership and society. In the course of the propaganda spree, the important fact that was altogether overlooked, deliberately or otherwise, was the gravity of concern and seriousness of practical steps that the Saudi leadership had respectively expressed and undertaken in response to the growing wave of international terrorism over the years, including the period prior to 11 September 2001.

Such concern was expressed, for instance, by King Abdullah bin Abdul Aziz (then Crown Prince), when he addressed the

United Nations Millennium Summit in September 2000. He said:

> The phenomenon of terrorism is still widespread in all parts of the world, although fluctuating considerably, and still requires greater effort from our organization in order to contain and combat it. The Government of the Kingdom of Saudi Arabia has always denounced all forms and shapes of terrorism and added its efforts to those of the international community to address the serious phenomenon. What should be emphasized in this respect is that extremism, violence and terrorism are a global phenomenon, not restricted to any people, race or religion. In view of the internationalism and comprehensiveness of this phenomenon, addressing and combating it effectively can only come through agreed upon international action within the framework of the United Nations, that ensures the elimination of terrorism, conservation of innocent life, and preservation of the supremacy and stability of the State.[4]

In so far as practical initiatives for stopping the growing wave of international terrorism which the Saudi leadership took are concerned, another proof that its counter-terrorism commitment predates the terrorist events of 11 September 2001, Saudi Arabia was the first member-state of the Organization of the Islamic Conference (OIC) to sign the Treaty on Combating International Terrorism in July 2000. On the occasion, Saudi Assistant Foreign Minister Dr Nizar Obaid Madani said that the move reflected the Kingdom's commitment to the teachings of Islamic Shariah, which rejects all kinds of violence, and its determination to combat the phenomenon of terrorism in all its forms, as well as its concern to strengthen cooperation among the OIC member states for the purpose.[5]

Saudi Arabia has taken a number of steps to combat terrorist financing in the aftermath of 11 September 2001, but its campaign against terrorist financing began long ago. Saudi Arabia was one of the first countries to take action against terrorist financing, freezing the assets of Osama bin Laden in 1994. In 1988, the Kingdom signed and joined the United Nations Convention against Illicit Trafficking of Narcotics and Psychotropic Substances. In 1995, Saudi Arabia established units countering money laundering at the Ministry of Interior, in the Saudi Arabian Monetary Agency (SAMA) and in the commercial banks. The same year, SAMA issued 'Guidelines for Prevention and Control of Money-Laundering Activities' to Saudi banks to implement 'Know your Customer' rules, maintain records of suspicious transactions, and report them to law enforcement officials and SAMA.[6]

Since 11 September 2001, Saudi Arabia has adopted a host of domestic measures to fight terrorism, including reforms in the country's administrative, educational, economic and financial sectors. The deep commitment to combating terrorism that exists at the highest level of Saudi leadership has helped the country to mobilize its various state organs and societal forces against terrorists. Islam is the founding principle of the Kingdom of Saudi Arabia, and, as discussion in the preceding chapter manifests clearly, Islam strictly forbids terrorist violence. Given that, the counter-terrorism discourse of the Saudi leadership is essentially grounded in Islamic precepts on the subject. In fact, in every speech that King Abdullah bin Abdul Aziz has made regarding the threat of terrorism and the ways to tackle it, he has made it a point to highlight the Islamic creed of peace, tolerance and brotherhood spanning all humanity. For instance, while addressing the 2003 OIC summit in Malaysia, he said:

> Islam is innocent of violence, hatred, and terrorism. It is a religion of kindness, mercy and tolerance. We should not allow a minority of deviant terrorists to tarnish its image. The bullets that kill women and children, terrorize those secured in their safety and destroy innocent communities, do not come from rifles, but from deviant thoughts and misguided interpretations of our great religion and its noble message.[7]

POLICY GUIDELINES

In order to make its fight against terrorism effective and viable, the Kingdom of Saudi Arabia has adopted a number of policy guidelines. These guidelines are an outcome of a realization on the part of the Saudi leadership that ignorance of Islamic precepts and the principal objectives of the Shariah, together with an inherent fanaticism of thought, constitute the primary reasons spurring terrorist activities.

The domestic policy guidelines include a firm stand based on the Islamic Shariah and the traditions of the holy Prophet

(PBUH), a commitment to countering terrorism in all its forms and manifestations, undertaking steps for creating an enabling environment for condemning terrorist activities in all walks of life, introducing an educational curriculum at all levels with emphasis on the primary principles of moderation and tolerance, extending moral and material assistance to security personnel entrusted with the task of countering terrorism, including financial assistance to such families that have suffered loss of life or property during their encounters with terrorists, and extending medical and financial support to all its citizens and residents who have been affected on account of terrorism to alleviate their sufferings.

THREE-PRONGED STRATEGY

Saudi Arabia has adopted a comprehensive strategy to counter terrorism, including military as well as non-military instruments. In addition to combating terrorism by force through stringent security and law-enforcement measures, the Saudi government has put in place an effective legal system to dissuade and punish terrorists, prevent terrorist financing through charitable donations and money laundering, besides undertaking a host of reforms in education, information and other social sectors. In addition to exercising the security option, Saudi Arabia has followed a three-pronged core strategy to combat terrorism, including Prevention, Cure and Care.

THE STRATEGY OF PREVENTION

The strategy of prevention is meant to extend support to efforts aimed at making the society understand the dangers of deviant thinking, encourage moderate thinking and rectify wrong concepts. A number of preventive measures have been adopted as part of this strategy, including encouraging religious scholars to publish books and produce audio cassettes to promote moderate thinking, organizing scholarly seminars, lectures and debates for the purpose, sponsoring media programmes aimed at explaining the dangers of deviant thinking and disseminating correct and moderate religious concepts, extending cooperation to educational institutions for propagating moderate thinking, correcting erroneous perceptions through interaction with students, and reviewing curricula and restructuring teaching faculties, emphasizing that there is no contradiction between Islamic identity and national identity, urging social institutions, including mosques, schools and families, to play their due role in countering deviant thinking, and urging citizens to counter the claims of deviant groups through the Internet and other means of dissemination.

THE STRATEGY OF CURE

Within the Ministry of Interior in Saudi Arabia, a group called the advisory committee administers the re-education and counselling programme. It comprises four sub-committees, which are:

1. **The Religious Scholars Sub-Committee**: Comprising of over one hundred clerics, scholars and university professors, the Religious Committee is tasked with initiating a dialogue with detainees to remove any doubts in their minds and holding courses on general topics concerning deviant thinking.

2. **The Social and Psychological Sub-Committee**: Comprising of around thirty social scientists, psychologists and researchers, its members are tasked with evaluating a prisoner's social status, diagnosing any psychological problems, assessing the prisoner's status and compliance during the process, and determining what support the prisoner and his family may need.

3. **The Security Sub-Committee**: It performs various tasks including evaluating prisoners for security risks, making release recommendations, advising prisoners on how to behave upon release, and monitoring prisoners and who they associate with once they leave prison.

4. **The Media Sub-Committee**: It reviews the content of programmes being transmitted by the media to ensure that there is nothing in there to mislead young minds, and also guides media persons about the parameters of desirable informative programmes. It is focused on outreach and education, targeting young Saudi men.

THE STRATEGY OF CARE

The primary purpose of this leg of the Saudi counter-terrorism strategy is coordination. Its efforts include interacting with those released from detention and their families, providing financial and moral support to former detainees and their families, initiating schemes to rehabilitate those released from detention and helping them re-adjust to the requirements of Saudi society and find jobs, settle down and get married.

The reform committees help to correct the false thinking of the detainees and urge them to comply with moderation as enshrined in Islam. This is implemented through the use of scientific and contemporary methodologies together with the initiation of a lengthy dialogue with those incarcerated. The principal aim of the reformists is to identify the reasons that led to errant thinking and bring across to them the true teachings of Islam and the *Sunnah* (the way and manners) of the holy Prophet (PBUH) through highly qualified religious teachers and scholars. Psychiatrists and sociologists are also included in these reformatory teams to provide due help to detainees. Members of the reform committees maintain regular contact with the families and relatives of the detainees, assuring them that their loved ones are taken care of and are being persuaded to adopt the true Islamic creed of peace and devotion to the welfare of society. This is accomplished through conducting courses in reconstruction of self-confidence and eliminating any psychological disorders.[8]

Members of the reform committees consisting of religious scholars, psychiatrists and sociologists meet often with the detainees to understand their mindset that has been tampered with by inculcating the hate syndrome, and to find ways and means to reform them into becoming good and productive members of society again. Those released from jail are constantly followed-up to ensure that they stay on the right path and do not resume their deviant ways. Healthy living conditions are provided to former detainees through monthly stipends. Assistance is also provided to those who are desirous of continuing their education at the school or university level. Psychological and social security are ensured through financial assistance for purposes of marriage, dowry, buying or renting accommodation, furnishing and conveyance as may be required. A special budget has been allocated for these purposes.[9]

MAIN DOMESTIC MEASURES

Since the 11 September 2001 terrorist events, and especially in response to a series of terrorist attacks against Saudi Arabia in subsequent years, the Saudi authorities have adopted several measures to tackle the terrorist wave. These include steps to regulate the work of charitable organizations and reforms in the country's banking and financial sectors to combat terrorist financing, reformative initiatives in the educational and information sectors to prevent deviant thinking, and stringent security and legal measures to nab terrorists and bring them to justice.

STEPS AGAINST TERRORIST FINANCING

Since 11 September 2001, the Saudi government has conducted a thorough review of its charitable organizations and has incorporated a number of significant changes. Under new government regulations, the measures that have been taken necessitate that all bank accounts of charitable or welfare societies are consolidated into a single account for each such society. The Saudi Arabia Monetary Association (SAMA) may give permission for a subsidiary account, if necessary, but such an account can only be used to receive, not to withdraw or transfer funds. Deposits in these accounts will be accepted only after the depositor provides the bank with identification and all other required information for verification. No ATM cards or credit cards can be issued for these accounts and no cash withdrawals are permitted from the charitable institution's account. All cheques and drafts are to be made in favour of legitimate beneficiaries and for deposit in a bank account only. No charitable or welfare society can open and operate these accounts without first presenting a valid copy of the required license, no overseas fund transfers are allowed from these bank accounts, and SAMA's approval is required to open a bank account. Only two individuals, duly authorized by the Board of a charitable institution, are allowed to operate the main account.[10]

In February 2004, a National Saudi Society for Relief and Charitable Works Abroad was established, which has allowed the government to exert more stringent oversight of Saudi charitable activities abroad. The government has taken fundamental steps to increase accountability and prevent misuse of the fundamental Islamic tenet of *zakat*, or charity, including the removal of all cash collection boxes from mosques and shopping centres. It has reined in the activities of *hawala*s, which are the informal money transfer services commonly used throughout the Arabian Gulf region, particularly by foreign workers. Independent *hawala*s are being closed down in the Kingdom and replaced with government-regulated establishments that perform essentially the same function, but with far greater oversight.[11]

A High Commission for oversight of all charities, contributions and donations has been established, along with operational procedures to manage and audit contributions and donations to and from the charities, including their work abroad. In May 2002, SAMA issued rules 'Governing the Opening of Bank Accounts' and 'General Operational Guidelines' in order to protect banks against money-laundering activities. For instance, Saudi banks are not permitted to open bank accounts for non-resident individuals without specific approval from SAMA. Banks are required to apply strict 'Know your Customer' rules and any non-customer business has to be fully documented.

In August 2003, the Saudi government began implementing new legislation that stipulated harsh penalties for the crime of money laundering and terror financing. The new law bans financial transactions with unidentified parties, requires banks to maintain records of transactions for up to ten years, allows intelligence units to investigate suspicious transactions, and ensures international cooperation on money laundering issues with countries with which formal agreements have been signed. In February 2003, SAMA initiated implementation of a major technical programme to train judges and investigators on terror financing and money laundering. The programme trains judges and investigators on legal matters involving terror financing and money laundering methods, international requirements for financial secrecy and the methods followed by criminals to exchange information.[12]

Special training programmes have been developed for bankers, prosecutors, judges, customs officers, and other officials from government departments and agencies. Furthermore, training programmes are offered by the Prince Naif Security Academy, King Fahd Security Faculty, Public Security Training City and SAMA. The Saudi government has established a permanent committee of representatives of seven ministries and government agencies to manage all legal and other issues related to money-laundering activities. The first conference for the Financial Action Task Force (FATF) outside the G-7 countries was held in Riyadh at the SAMA Institute of Banking in 1994. In January 2002, SAMA organized, in cooperation with law enforcement agencies, banking and financial institutions, and Interpol's Riyadh office, the First Asian Regional Conference of Interpol. In May 2002, the Council of Saudi Chambers of Commerce and Industry, in cooperation with SAMA, conducted an International Conference on Prevention and Detection of Fraud, Economic Crimes, and Money Laundering.[13]

The Saudi legislative, regulatory and supervisory framework for banking and financial services ensures that each bank or financial service provider remains vigilant with strong internal controls, processes and procedures to not only know the identity of its customers, but also have awareness of their activities and transactions. SAMA and the Ministry of Commerce issued instructions and guidelines to the Kingdom's financial and commercial sectors for combating money-laundering activities. To further strengthen and implement the current regulations, the Ministry of Commerce issued Regulation No. 1312 aimed at preventing and combating money laundering in the non-financial sector. These regulations are aimed at manufacturing and trading sectors and also cover professional services such as accounting, legal affairs, and consultancy. SAMA has instructed Saudi banks to establish supervisory committees to closely monitor the threat posed by terrorism and to coordinate all efforts to freeze the assets of the identified individuals and entities. For this purpose, Saudi banks have also put in place, at the level of their Chief Executive Officers, as well as that of the supervisory committees, mechanisms to respond to all relevant enquiries, both domestic and international.[14]

The Saudi government has created an institutional framework for combating money laundering including the establishment of special units, which work in coordination with SAMA and law enforcement agencies. The government has also encouraged banks to bring money laundering related experiences to the notice of various bank committees (such as Fraud Committees, and those of Chief Operations Officers and Managing Directors) for exchange of information and joint action.[15]

Saudi banks and SAMA have implemented an online reporting system to identify trends in money-laundering activities to assist in policymaking and other related initiatives. Another major institutional initiative is the creation of a specialized Financial Intelligence Unit (FIU) in the Security and Drug Control Department of the Ministry of Interior. This unit is specially tasked with handling money-laundering cases. The government carries out regular inspections of banks to ensure compliance with laws and regulations. Any violation or non-compliance is cause for serious action and is referred to a bank's senior management and the Board. Furthermore, the Government has created a permanent committee of banks' compliance officers to review regulations and guidelines, recommend improvements, and ensure that all implementation issues are resolved.[16]

Since institutionalizing counter-terrorist financing reforms in the banking and financial sectors, the Saudi authorities have investigated many bank accounts suspected of having links to terrorism, and by December 2002, had frozen thirty-three accounts belonging to three individuals that totalled $5,574,196. Since then, more of such accounts worth millions of dollars have been frozen. For instance, in September 2002, in a joint action by the United States Treasury Department and the Saudi government, the assets of Wa'el Hamza Julaidan, an associate of Osama bin Laden who provided financial and logistical support to al-Qaeda, were frozen.

Acknowledging the importance of Saudi steps against terrorist financing, J. Cofer Black, US State Department's Coordinator for Counter-terrorism,[17] said the US,

> dialogue with the Saudis on counter-terrorism issues has grown closer over the past year. This effort has included a number of initiatives to stop terrorist financing and bolster law enforcement and intelligence cooperation. Counter-terrorism finance has been the central focus of the government-to-government engagement. The Saudis have responded with an impressive array of new institutional, legal and regulatory changes aimed at combating terrorist finance. Saudi officials are making the changes to financial and charity systems, which will choke off the flow of funds that keep al-Qaeda and other terrorists in business.

SECURITY AND LEGAL STEPS

A stringent domestic security system is an effective hedge against the terrorist threat at home and its external manifestations. Apart from developing such a system, Saudi intelligence and law enforcement authorities have worked closely with the United States and other countries as well as with Interpol to identify, question and, whenever appropriate, arrest terrorist suspects.

The Saudi establishment's effort to counter terrorism is motivated by three inter-related objectives, including fighting terrorists with force, arresting them beforehand, and bringing them to justice though a court trial. In recent years, Saudi security services investigated thousands of suspected terrorists, and arrested hundreds of alleged al-Qaeda collaborators. In the aftermath of the May and November 2003 terrorist bombings, for instance, the Saudi law enforcement authorities arrested more than 600 terror suspects.[18] The authorities have conducted several raids against al-Qaeda cells and terrorist operatives allegedly using Saudi territory for terrorist operations at home and abroad. The security forces have suffered casualties in these raids. However, through these raids, Saudi security and law-enforcement agencies have been able to seize sizeable caches of explosives and ammunition, and hunt down terror suspects.

As of December 2006, the Saudi authorities had questioned thousands of suspects and arrested more than 800 individuals with suspected ties to terrorism.[19] Since then, hundreds of additional suspects have been arrested. During the court trial, many of these suspects have repented their terrorist actions. Among those were religious clerics who, through their sermons, had tried to promote deviant learning, and thus, fuel terrorism. Some of them, during their time in prison, repented their deeds. This happened largely due to their interaction with members of reform committees. For instance, after the May 2003 Riyadh bombings, three clerics, Ali Fahd al Khudair, Ahmed Hamoud Mufreh al Khaledi, and Nasir Ahmed al Fuhaid, were arrested, since they had called for support of the terrorists who carried out these bombings. By the end of the year, all of these clerics had appeared on Saudi state television, recanting and withdrawing their previous religious opinions and describing them as 'grave mistakes'.[20]

The Saudi government's pre-emptive strategies to dry up sources of terrorist funding, as well as the growing security awareness of Saudi citizens, have led to the surrender of militants. Security officials have released recorded statements made by members of terror cells to be used on prime time television broadcasts. All of them described how they had been convinced by preachers who issued edicts forbidding Muslims from working with the Saudi government, demanded that Muslims work to rid the Arabian Peninsula of non-Muslims, and declared that any Muslim who did not share these views was an infidel. One of the men said during his taped statement: 'Thank God, I was jailed and God enlightened me'.[21]

The use of the criminal justice system can help reduce terrorism in several ways. The prospect of being caught and punished may deter other terrorists from attacking in the first place. Even if not deterred, the movement of terrorists still at large can be impeded by knowledge that they are wanted men. The drama and publicity of a criminal trial may also help to sustain public support for counter-terrorism, demonstrate the government's resolve to go after terrorists, and encourage other governments to do the same. For instance, the new Saudi law that came into force in August 2003 puts in place harsh penalties for money laundering and terror financing, including jail sentences of up to fifteen years and fines up to $1.8 million for offenders.[22]

SOCIAL SECTOR REFORMS

Besides adopting stringent security measures and strict legal steps criminalizing terrorism, the Saudi government has attempted to counter terrorism effectively by reforming the education sector on modern lines, and using the media to mould public opinion against terrorists justifying their actions by using deviant thinking. In recent years, Saudi education and information institutions have undergone extensive reforms. The guiding spirit behind these reforms has been the consistent campaign by the leading Saudi authorities on Islam about the un-Islamic and inhuman nature of terrorist violence, whatever its root causes may be. The campaign aims to clarify to the people, inside and outside Saudi Arabia, that Islam is a religion of peace, has no place for terrorism, and stands for brotherhood among all human beings.

In May 2003, after the bombings in Riyadh, the Saudi Ministry of Islamic Affairs announced the removal of 353 religious officials from their positions because they lacked the 'qualifications' to work in mosques, and the requirement that 1,357 religious officials undergo further training.[23] Immediately after 11 September 2001, leading Saudi religious officials condemned the attacks and, since then, have consistently and publicly rejected bin Laden's interpretation of jihad. Another example was the August 2003 statement of the Higher Council of *Ulama* (religious scholars), reaffirming that violent attacks on innocents 'are criminal acts, not jihad in the path of God'. The council called on the Saudi authorities to bring before the courts any scholar who issues a *fatwa* (edict) approving of such acts.[24]

Sheikh Abdul Aziz Al-Asheikh, the Grand Mufti of Saudi Arabia, continues to issue statements emphasizing that any Muslim who is aware of the teachings of his religion and who adheres to the holy Qur'an and the *Sunnah* will never involve himself in terrorist attacks or sympathize with the kidnapping and killing of innocent people. The danger, according to him, is not only from the terrorists themselves, but also from those who sympathize with them and make it possible for the terrorists to carry out their savage actions. Likewise, the Imams at the Grand Mosque in Makkah and at the holy Prophet's (PBUH) Mosque in Madinah continue to preach tolerance and warn against terrorism and extremism in their Friday sermons. In the words of Sheikh Saleh Bin-Humaid, 'every act of sabotage targeting peaceful citizens and residents who are under Saudi Arabia's protection is forbidden and is against the Shariah. Muslims should not accept any justification for such behaviour, no matter where it came from'. According to Sheikh Ali ibn Abdul Rahman, Imam at the holy Prophet's (PBUH) Mosque, 'kidnapping non-Muslims and killing them is a heinous crime which amounts to treason against Islam and a betrayal of what it teaches'.[25]

THE RELIGIOUS POLICE

Scholars in the Imam Mohammad ibn Saud Islamic University are engaged in a comprehensive research on the causes of terrorism. The Commission for the Promotion of Virtue and

Prevention of Vice, known as the *mutawwa*s or the religious police, is an integral part of the Saudi social fabric, and its job is essentially to ensure that Islamic morals and behaviour are followed in public and in private.

The Commission has established a programme aimed at upgrading and improving the qualifications of its members. An Academy of Islamic Police at Umm Al-Qura University in Makkah has been established to qualify students to be better guardians and role models of Islamic virtues. The curriculum does not concentrate on Islamic studies alone, but also teaches psychology and English.

The Saudi government has sponsored a number of symposia, its officials have participated in conferences and conducted dialogue with intellectuals, politicians and religious figures.[26]

THE MEDIA

The Saudi media is engaged in an aggressive campaign against extremists and al-Qaeda sympathizers in the Kingdom. The local press and electronic media regularly illustrates the public resentment of extremists and Saudi society's condemnation of targeting foreigners as well as all other terrorist acts.

The media has further involved itself in the continuing debate between moderates and hardliners. It continues to publicize and expose certain deviant interpretations of Islam that have led some Muslims to resort to violence. The heroism of the security forces is covered extensively with commentaries and editorials reflecting public support for them and condemnation of acts of terrorism and violence. Journalists continue to promote moderation and tolerance and well-known writers are highly critical of the extremist ideology espoused by some members of society.

The Saudi Media and Communications Association is busy reaching out to the West in order to clarify misconceptions about Islam and present accurate information about Saudi Arabia's active role in combating terrorism.[27]

REFORM PROGRAMME IN PRISONS

Saudi Arabia was one of the first countries in the Arab world to set up professional and comprehensive reform programmes in prisons. In mid-2004, Saudi Arabian authorities initiated *al-Munasaha wa al-Islah* (Advice and Reform) with the aim of targeting certain individuals who were detained on terrorism-related charges. The 'de-radicalization' and rehabilitation programme was started after the wave of terrorist attacks in May and November 2003, and it was only one of a number of counter-terrorism tactics adopted as part of the general counter-terrorism strategy by the Kingdom. To implement and promote the programme, the Saudi government established a special committee. The Saudi move was based on the belief that the great majority of young people who had been detained were victims of misguided interpretations of Islam, or had succumbed to pressure from the militant groups.[28]

Therefore, the programme aimed to gain the trust of prisoners, and enlighten them on the true teachings of Islam, which forbid followers from using violence against civilian Muslims or non-Muslims. The programme presented alternatives for those who were willing to review their attitude and change. The initial run of the programme encountered some difficulties as prisoners mistrusted the authorities and disbelieved the promises and intentions of the project managers and consultants from the official religious institutions. Terrorist groups also worked hard to discredit the programme and publicly warned anybody working with the project. Yet, the programme was successful and Saudi officials confirm that only 3 to 5 per cent of the hard-line prisoners from 2004 to 2007 relapsed into their old ways.[29]

Numerous factors have contributed to the success of the programme.[30] The programme targets Islamists who have not yet committed a terrorist act, but have shown an inclination to become involved in terrorist activities. It is, therefore, easier to convince these Islamists that their ideas and actions were wrongly perceived. Many of the detainees did not have a proper and adequate understanding of the holy Qur'an and were surprised by the interpretation provided by the religious scholars who visited them in prison.

The Saudi government made a huge financial commitment of over $30 million for the programme from 2004 to 2007 alone. The programme provides social and economic incentives for detainees who decide to cooperate. As part of the incentives, employment and houses were provided. Even marriages for the detainees were arranged in the belief that responsibility for a family would prevent the detainees from being attracted to the militant cause.

The Ministry of Interior, and not the Ministry of Religious Affairs, oversees *al-Munasaha wa al-Islah* in Saudi Arabia. This is important as only the Ministry of Interior has the authority to give security guarantees to the detainees promising that if they cooperate, it would not only provide them with benefits, but would also recommend their release from prison. Based on such recommendations, the Saudi government has already released more than 1,000 prisoners, which is a matter of encouragement for other prisoners to cooperate.

In spite of the soft approach of the programme, the prisoners are well aware of the consequences if they fail to cooperate with the programme's objective.

The success of the Saudi reform programme contributed to official responses from other countries. In 2003, the government in Yemen established the committee of *al-Hawar al-Fikri* (the intellectual dialogue) headed by an Islamic religious scholar. The scholar confirmed that within a few months of the start of the programme, the government agreed to free some detainees on the recommendation of the committee. In 2004, the number of detainees freed as part of the programme increased substantially and there are growing reasons to believe that the programme will contribute to the emergence of a terror-free society in the future.

THE BATTLE OF THE INTERNET

As part of the battle to win hearts and minds in Saudi Arabia, an initiative has also been undertaken to tackle the influence of the radicals over the Internet. In 2004, a number of religious scholars set up a web page under the name *Sakeenah* (inner peace) to fight terrorism at an ideological level. The web page offered open debates and responded to questions asked.

In October 2000, the Presidency for Scientific Research and Religious Edicts (*Dar al-Ift'a*), a Riyadh based organization comprising prominent Islamic scholars that issues *fatwa*s, set up a website for its religious rulings. The site provides access to *fatwa*s issued by *Dar al-Ift'a,* which is affiliated with the Council of Senior Islamic Scholars of Saudi Arabia headed by the Grand Mufti.

The decision to tackle radical ideology over the Internet was made after it was alleged that some *Imams* in Saudi Arabia were issuing *fatwa*s and calling on young people to take part in jihad. The project also aims to tackle the broadening jihadist Internet scene that increasingly targets and recruits vulnerable young people through the worldwide web.

By undertaking such comprehensive reforms in the domestic security, legal, administrative, financial and societal sectors, the Saudi government has been able to combat terrorism at home considerably. The Kingdom has, indeed, employed force against terrorists, but only to prevent a real terrorist threat from materializing. However, as is clear from the above-mentioned policy guidelines and the three-pronged strategy, its overall counter-terrorism strategy at home is geared towards finding a long-term solution to the problem of terrorism through a wide-ranging institutional and societal level reforms process.

MANIFESTATIONS OF SUCCESS

It is generally acknowledged that, within a short span of time, the Saudi counter-terrorism strategy has yielded positive results not only in terms of effectively combating terrorism, but also with regard to preventing its occurrence by working with those who have a destructive mindset.

Since the launching of the programme, more than 3,000 persons have participated in the counselling programme. More than 90 per cent of them have renounced their former beliefs and have been released. They are now living a normal life like other peaceful Saudi citizens. Some are still incarcerated as they are undergoing treatment and rehabilitation. It is expected that they would also renounce their deviant ways and would return to living a healthy and non-violent life. Of course, there have been a few cases of former prisoners undergoing rehabilitation who later reverted to extremist activities. However, the vast majority of such cases have resumed normal life after undergoing the de-radicalization experience, which proves the effectiveness and relevance of the Saudi counter-terrorism strategy.[31]

The vast array of people who have been guided to renounce their extremist views also include religious scholars. They have appeared on state television and invoked their disciples to purge themselves of extremist and violent leanings and take to a life of moderation. This has provided motivation for people in general, belonging to all walks of life, to re-think their beliefs and organize them in accordance with the moderate principles enshrined in Islam and its teachings.

The success of the Saudi domestic counter-terrorism approach is also being increasingly acknowledged by the Western media and academia. Recent works by Rachael Rudolph and N.P. Tollitz underline the growing resolve of the Saudi authorities to combat terrorism with a mix of short-term and long-term approaches, in response to the increasing threat from the al-Qaeda-led terrorism against the Kingdom in recent years.[32]

In his report 'Saudi Arabia's "Soft" Counter-Terrorism Strategy: Prevention, Rehabilitation, and Aftercare', Christopher Boucek says:

> The counselling programme and counter-radicalization strategies in the Kingdom highlight several factors that will be essential in any effort to demobilize militants. The involvement and treatment of an individual's family and extended social network are central to successful demobilization. Research on the Saudi programme has shown that participants develop intense relationships with the sheikhs and scholars with whom they interact during the dialogues. The majority will leave detention as very religious and observant Muslims. This is to be expected since many initially become involved with extremists in an attempt to become more religious.[33]

The report goes on to say:

> In today's dangerous environment, interest in rehabilitation
> programme is certain to intensify and more nations will seek to
> implement programmes modelled after Saudi Arabia's. Though
> started in 2004, the Saudi operation is the most expansive, best
> funded and longest continuously running counter-radicalization
> programme in existence. When Singapore developed a
> programme to combat extremism, its approach was based in part
> on the Saudi model. The strategy employed by the US Marine
> Corps in its Task Force 134 'House of Wisdom' project which
> deals with insurgent Iraqi detainees, was devised, in turn, with
> advice from Singaporean officials. In only a few years' time,
> Saudi Arabia's soft strategy to combat extremism and terrorism
> has generated some very promising results. It warrants greater
> evaluation especially as other nations struggling with extremism
> look at what is being accomplished in the Kingdom for lessons
> they can employ in their homelands. Throughout the Middle
> East, Europe and Asia, similar programmes are starting to
> emerge. That other nations emulate the Saudi programme is
> ultimately based on the recognition that the defeat of extremism
> cannot be achieved through hard security measures alone. That,
> in itself, is a major accomplishment.[34]

This comment is generally reflective of not only a
comprehensive approval of the dynamics of the Saudi anti-
terrorism programme, but also its acceptability in other
countries of the world and a desire to model it to suit their
domestic needs and requirements. In fact, there are already

examples of countries which have made use of the Saudi approach with effective and far-reaching results.

A recent report in *The New York Times* says:

In January 2009, the Saudi Kingdom released a list of wanted terrorist suspects, all 85 of them were said to be outside the Kingdom. That fact was a measure of the ambitious Saudi counterterrorism programme in the past few years. The government has cracked down ruthlessly on terrorist cells and financing, rooting out officers with extremist sympathies and building a much larger and more effective network of SWAT teams. Even regular police officers now get a full month of counter-terrorism training every year. The post-prison rehabilitation programme, which is now being expanded, is only one part of a broader effort to address the issue of violent extremism across Saudi Arabia. It includes dialogues with, or even suppression of, the more extremist clerics. There are also a variety of outreach programmes in areas known to harbour extremists, with the Interior Ministry sending its preferred clerics or sheikhs to speak in schools and community centres for two or three weeks at a time. At the same time, the kingdom has completely retooled its prison system, which had been criticized as having inhumane conditions. Five new prisons were built in a matter of months in 2008 that hold 1,200 to 1,500 prisoners each. Unlike the old prisons, the new ones allow a maximum of four inmates to a cell, and Islamists are kept separate from common criminals for the first time, minimizing the spread of jihadist ideas.[35]

In July 2008, *The Economist* commented:

Saudi authorities seemed to have got a firm grip on the militants. Their policy mixed hard-nosed security operations and an extensive de-radicalization programme in the prisons with social measures for the families of militants. Today, Saudi Arabia, often considered the fount of hardline ideology and finance for jihadists, is seen by many as a model for fighting terrorism. For the past three years, al-Qaeda in Saudi Arabia appears to have become increasingly fragmented, with no clear leadership or methodology. Alms-giving and money transfers, the main sources of terrorist funding, have been restricted to a point where some Western diplomats say it could drive all charitable donations underground and become counterproductive. *Sawt al-Jihad* (Voice of Jihad), one of the best-known jihadi online magazines, disappeared for more than two years. Official propaganda talks of extremists as 'misguided' or 'deviant'. Those due for release after serving short sentences for, say, fighting in Iraq, undergo rehabilitation in a low-security holiday camp outside Riyadh. Other inmates have served time at Guantánamo Bay. The young men spend their days in religious discussions, art therapy, sports, vocational training and psychological assessments. Inmates on rehabilitation are encouraged to reconnect with friends and family on frequent home visits. When they leave, the state gives them money if they have no job, helps them find work, buys them a car and even assists them in finding a wife. Family members are looked after, too, to ensure they are not recruited by extremists. Friends, relatives and tribal elders are enlisted to ensure good behaviour.[36]

The success of the de-radicalization programme has led to numerous visible changes that can be noted in day-to-day life in Saudi Arabia. The security presence that had increased after the 9/11 attacks in the US has reduced considerably, by 50 per cent according to some estimates. Security checks are gradually being done away with in the wake of peace and calm having returned to the Kingdom.

Other factors that have contributed significantly to the success of the Saudi counter-terrorism strategy include the creation of sizeable job opportunities in the Kingdom as a result of the broad-based industrial and development projects that have been launched by the government. This has generated a feeling of hope among the people who can now look forward to a successful, financially stable and rewarding life. That has, consequently, reduced the prospects of the youth from being infected with extremist invective.

Though the Saudi de-radicalization process is only five years old, its success is also demonstrated by the increasing interest that a lot of countries are taking in it and adapting it to suit their domestic needs. The case of Indonesia that has been discussed in detail later in the book is one such example. There are other cases, and there would be more as countries and leaderships recognize the difference that the Saudi de-radicalization strategy is making to the world in terms of improving the security situation as well as keeping people from falling into the trap of extremist and deviant minds.

Today, Saudi Arabia stands cleansed of practically all religious rhetoric. Because of stringent laws and policies introduced by the government, there is little prospect that anyone with extremist leanings would be able to misuse the mosque or other places of religious congregations for advancing the cause of terrorism and militancy. Strict control is kept on the activities and interactions of those who are even remotely suspected of espousing the cause of extremism. This approach renders them practically ineffective and prone to renouncing their leanings and tilting towards a life of moderation.

NOTES

1. See the statement in *Post-September 11 Scenarios: The Efforts of the Embassy of Saudi Arabia, Pakistan, to Combat Terrorism* (Islamabad: Embassy of the Kingdom of Saudi Arabia, 2005), p. 21.
2. For details about the incident, see Yaroslav Trofimov, *The Siege of Makkah: The Forgotten Uprising* (New York: Penguin, 2007).
3. Brig.-Gen. Ahmed S. Al-Mufarih, *The Role of the Kingdom of Saudi Arabia in Combating Terrorism*, USAWC Strategy Research Project (Carlisle Barracks, Penn.: US Army War College, 3 May 2004).
4. See official website of the Ministry of Foreign Affairs, Kingdom of Saudi Arabia, http://www.mofa.gov.sa/detail.asp?InServiceID=205& intemplatekey=MainPage, accessed on 15 May 2008.
5. Ibid.
6. Anthony H. Cordesman, *Saudi Arabia Enters the Twenty-First Century: The Political, Foreign Policy, Economic, and Energy Dimensions* (Westport, Conn: Praeger, 2003), pp. 217–219.
7. See the speech at official website of the OIC, http://www.oic-oci. org/ex-summit/english/speeches/king-speech-sum.htm
8. Al-Mufarih, op. cit.
9. Ibid.
10. Cordesman, op. cit.

11. *Saudi Arabia and the Fight against Terrorist Financing*, testimony of J. Cofer Black, Coordinator for Counter-terrorism, US Department of State, to the Middle East and Central Asia Subcommittee of the House International Relations Committee, 24 March 2004.

12. Ibid., pp. 19–21.

13. Al-Mufarih, op. cit.

14. Ibid., op. cit.

15. Cordesman, op. cit.

16. Ibid., op. cit.

17. *Saudi Arabia and the Fight against Terrorist Financing*, op. cit.

18. Neil MacFarquhar, 'Al Qaeda Blamed in Deadly Attack on Saudi Homes,' *The New York Times*, 10 November 2003.

19. For details about the arrested terrorist suspects during 2002–2006, see *Initiatives and Actions Taken by the Kingdom of Saudi Arabia in the War on Terrorism* (Washington, DC: Royal Embassy of Saudi Arabia, December 2006). Available from www.saudiembassy.net, accessed 15 May 2008.

20. Ibid.

21. Samar Fatany, 'Combating Terrorism and Extremism in Saudi Arabia, *Arab News*, 7 December 2004.

22. Al-Mufarih, op. cit.

23. *Al-Hayat*, 28 May 2003.

24. Ibid., 17 August 2003.

25. Fatany, op. cit.

26. Ibid.

27. Ibid.

28. Nicole Stracke, 'Arab Prisons: A Place for Dialogue and Reform,' *Perspectives on Terrorism*, Vol. 1, No. 4 (2007).

29. Ibid.

30. Ibid. Also see *Al-Riyadh*, 9 December 2005 and *Al Sharq Al Awsat*, 21 April 2007.

31. In January 2009, the Saudi government released a list of eighty-five suspects, which included eleven men who had been freed from Guantanamo Bay. They had passed through the Saudi rehabilitation programme, and had then fled the country. Two of them broadcast their aim of overthrowing the Saudi royal family in a video released on the Internet by the Yemeni branch of Al-Qaeda. This was no doubt embarrassing for the Saudi government. However, *The New York Times* says the Saudi government is now 'far more open about the challenges it faces.' The paper quotes Turki al-Otayan, the director of the rehabilitation programme's psychological committee, as saying 'We are still at the beginning, we have a lot to learn'....but the success rate (14 failures out of 218 graduates) was still impressive. See Robert F. Worth, 'Saudis Retool to Root Out Terrorist Risk,' *The New York Times*, 21 March 2009.

32. Rachael M. Rudolph, *Saudi Arabia's War on Terrorism: From 1929 to 2003* (VDM Verlag, 2009). N.P. Tollitz, ed., *Saudi Arabia, US Relations and Oil* (Nova Science Publishers, Inc., 2005).

33. Christopher Boucek, *Saudi Arabia's 'Soft' Counter-Terrorism Strategy: Prevention, Rehabilitation and Aftercare*, Carnegie Papers (Washington, DC: Carnegie Endowment for International Peace, September 2008), pp. 22–23.

34. Ibid.

35. Worth, op. cit.

36. 'Powers of Persuasion,' *The Economist*, 17 July 2008.

6

Saudi Strategy against Terrorism: International Initiatives

In addition to tackling terrorism at home through a multi-faceted counter-terrorism approach, Saudi Arabia has supported numerous regional and international efforts in the fight against terrorism through bilateral and multi-lateral agreements. The Saudi government works closely with the United Nations, the United States and the European Union, besides a number of other countries and international and regional organizations concerned about the threat of international terrorism, to exchange and share with them any counter-terrorism information quickly and effectively so that a possible future terrorist act is prevented from happening.

POLICY GUIDELINES

The Saudi counter-terrorism policy guidelines, as they apply to the international level, include fighting terrorism locally in cooperation with international partners and joining the international community in condemning terrorism as a global threat, endorsing the protocols to fight terrorism at the regional level, endorsing a unified security strategy of Gulf Cooperation Council (GCC) countries to confront extremism and terrorism, condemning terrorism at the UN General Assembly sessions and a firm commitment to fully support all its resolutions related to countering terrorism and signing of bilateral accords with friendly countries in the framework of security collaboration.

These policy guidelines further include cooperating and coordinating with all Arab countries and other friendly countries for countering terrorism, including exchanging information, expertise and technical assistance for countering crimes and activities of terrorist groups, their leadership, the places of their concentration, their training, the sources of their funding and armaments, the types of their weapons, ammunition and explosives, the means of communication and propagation in the use of such terrorist groups, their *modus operandi*, the movement of their leadership and types of travel documents used, exchanging data and information with friendly countries about plans of terrorist groups against the interests of other countries and their citizens. The practical manifestation of such international cooperation on the part of Saudi Arabia is quite obvious.

BILATERAL COOPERATION

Since the terrorist events of 11 September 2001, Saudi Arabia and the United States have closely cooperated with each other in combating terrorism. This cooperation is visible at various levels of relationship and in a number of important areas, including intelligence sharing, joint investigation and operation, and strategies to combat terrorist financing. In

August 2003, Saudi Arabia and the United States established
a Joint Task Force aimed at combating the financing of
terrorism. The establishment of the Saudi–US Task Force to
counter terrorist financing was proof of the importance that
King Abdullah bin Abdul Aziz (then Crown Prince of the
Kingdom) attached to combating terrorism through the
country's close cooperation with friendly countries. The
commissioning of the Saudi–US Task Force, incorporating
their law enforcement and intelligence agencies, enabled them
to share 'real time' intelligence and conduct joint operations
in the fight against terrorism. The Joint Task Force on
Terrorism Finance has helped move much of Saudi–US day-
to-day and case-by-case efforts in the 'War on Terror' away
from the interactions of diplomats and managed it on an
expeditious, real-time, law enforcement basis.[1]

The Saudi government has also conducted joint operations
with the United States and other friendly governments in
blocking the funds of suspected terrorist organizations.[2] In
January 2004, the Saudi government, in agreement with the
United States, submitted the names of four branches of the
Riyadh-based al-Haramain Foundation Charity to the UN
1267 Sanctions Committee for worldwide sanctions,
including asset freezing. As of 2004, the addition of these four
entities made for ten joint US–Saudi submissions to the UN
1267 Sanctions Committee since December 2002, the largest
number of joint designations with any country over that span.
Since then, the two countries have continued to work together
on preventing entities and individuals from providing

financial support to al-Qaeda.[3] Since April 2005, a Saudi–US Joint Commission for Strategic Dialogue has been underway. Its six working groups dealing with counter-terrorism, military affairs, economic and financial affairs, consular affairs and partnership, education exchange and human development in the US and Saudi Arabia have met a number of times.

Saudi cooperation with the United States and other countries as well as international security institutions such as Interpol in terms of law enforcement, the military and intelligence sharing, has intensified over time. The Saudi authorities, for instance, successfully negotiated with Iran for the extradition of some sixteen suspected al-Qaeda members. The Saudi government has, likewise, requested Interpol to arrest some 750 individuals, many of whom are suspected of money laundering, drug trafficking, and terror-related activities. This figure includes 214 Saudis, whose names appear in Interpol's database, in addition to expatriates who fled Saudi Arabia. Recently, the government of Saudi Arabia has issued another list of eighty-five terrorists and requested Interpol and the international community to extend help and support in their arrest.

The Saudi government has concluded several extradition agreements with friendly countries to locate and extradite al-Qaeda operatives allegedly hiding there. Dozens of citizens of other countries caught inside Saudi Arabia have been extradited to their respective countries, and vice versa.[4]

MULTILATERAL COOPERATION

As a member of G-20, Saudi Arabia proposed an aggressive plan of action directed at rooting out and freezing terrorist assets worldwide. After the proposed plan was approved by the G-20 countries, Saudi Arabia played a leading role in its implementation. In September 2003, a team of assessors from the Financial Action Task Force (FATF) and the Gulf Cooperation Council (GCC) visited the Kingdom. FATF is a multilateral organization of thirty-three members, individually and collectively devoted to combating money laundering. The FATF/GCC team conducted a formal assessment of Saudi Arabia's system of anti-money laundering and counter-terrorism finance laws and regulations, and the overarching supervisory and regulatory framework. Their February 2004 report documents that the Kingdom is in compliance or near-compliance with international standards in almost every indicator of effective instruments to combat money laundering and terrorist financing. While significant work remains, particularly in the area of implementation, this FATF/GCC report is a testament to the advances the Saudi government has made in shoring up its controls over its banking system and charities.[5]

Saudi Arabia has consistently supported international efforts to combat terrorism. It has signed a multilateral agreement under the auspices of the Arab League to confront terrorism. The Saudi government has signed various bilateral agreements with non-Arab countries to jointly fight the scourge. Every ninety days, it prepares and submits to various

United Nations Security Council Committees, upon request, a report on the initiatives and actions taken by the Kingdom with respect to the fight against terrorism. Over the years, the Saudi government has complied with all the United Nations resolutions relating to combating terrorism. The steps taken have included freezing funds and other financial assets of the Taliban regime based on UN Security Council Resolution 1267, freezing funds of listed individuals based on UN Security Council Resolution 1333, signing the International Convention for Suppression and Financing of Terrorism based on UN Security Council Resolution 1373, reporting to the UN Security Council the implementation of Resolution 1390 and extending support and implementing Resolution 1368 relating to the financing of terrorist activities.[6]

CONFERENCE ON COUNTERING TERRORISM

In a bid to realize an international consensus on the gravity of the threat posed by terrorism and to seek a genuine global input in tackling the widespread terrorist wave, the government of Saudi Arabia organized an International Conference on Combating Terrorism in Riyadh on 5–8 February 2005. Delegates from more than fifty countries and several representatives from international and regional organizations participated in the international event, which was aimed at achieving the objectives of highlighting the Kingdom's role in fighting terrorism, deliberating the concept of terrorism, its history, forms and root causes, discussing the relationship between terrorism, drug trafficking, weapons smuggling, and money laundering, and learning about various countries' experiences in countering terrorism, drawing practical lessons from their experiences, and helping the conference participants to apply these lessons in their respective countries' or organizations' efforts towards combating terrorism.

The first of its kind organized by any country, the February 2005 conference helped devise a long-term international strategy to counter terrorism as well as enhance the level of cooperation among various countries for the purpose.

In his inaugural speech on the occasion, King Abdullah bin Abdul Aziz (then Crown Prince of the Kingdom) said that the convening of the conference, which included nations from various cultures, faiths and political systems, was a,

> clear testimony that terrorism, when it strikes its victims, does not differentiate between cultures, faiths or forms of government. Terrorism does not belong to any culture, or religion, or political system. It is a global crime perpetrated by evil minds filled with hatred towards humanity and consumed with a blind desire to kill and destroy. This conference represents the will of the international community to combat this crime in every aspect by fighting evil with justice, confronting deviant thought with wisdom and noble ideas, and challenging extremism with moderation and tolerance.

In his speech, the Saudi King proposed the establishment of an International Centre for Combating Terrorism where experts in the area could 'exchange information instantly in response to the demands of the situation and the need to prevent incidents—God willing—before they occur'.[7]

The conference concluded with the Riyadh Declaration, which stressed that no international effort would be capable of effective confrontation with the phenomenon of terrorism unless there is cooperation and a comprehensive strategic perspective to deal with it. It supported the establishment of the International Centre for Combating Terrorism, as proposed by the Saudi leader. The Riyadh Declaration also stressed that the United Nations is the basic platform for the enhancement of international cooperation against terrorism, that the relevant UN Security Council resolutions form a firm and comprehensive basis for combating terrorism internationally, and that all countries should fully comply with these resolutions. It called on all countries to join, ratify and implement the twelve international treaties on combating terrorism.[8]

THE OIC INITIATIVE

Apart from reaching out to the wider world community for generating international consensus on the causes of terrorism, the threat it poses and strategies to address this threat—which was the main purpose behind the International Conference on Combating Terrorism—Saudi Arabia has attempted to use the Organization of Islamic Conference (OIC), the Muslim world's largest representative organization, to realize a collective Muslim world response to the danger of international terrorism. Since the founding of the OIC in 1969, the

Kingdom has played a leading role in its affairs, whether they pertain to the resolution of conflicts in the Muslim world such as Palestine or the adoption of political, economic, social, scientific and technological measures to revamp the Muslim world and put it on a modernist course. The international terrorist wave that has gripped the world in the concluding years of the twentieth century and at the beginning of the twenty-first century has a particular relevance for all Muslim countries, as in this terrorist wave the principal actors have somehow turned out to be a minority of individuals and organizations subscribing to a deviant religious creed that has nothing to do with the principles of Islam. It is no surprise, therefore, that the Saudi leadership has tried in recent years to use its traditional clout in the OIC in transforming the body into a principal Muslim world platform for combating terrorism in cooperation with the rest of the world.[9]

Towards this end, in January 2005, a month before organizing the International Conference on Combating Terrorism, King Abdullah bin Abdul Aziz (then Crown Prince of the Kingdom) called for the holding of an Extraordinary Islamic Summit for 'Meeting Challenges of the 21st Century' at Makkah in December 2005. On 9–11 September 2005, a Forum of Muslim Scholars and Intellectuals Preparatory to the Extraordinary Summit, consisting of over 100 persons representing various disciplines and hailing from countries within and outside the OIC, met at Makkah. It examined the challenges facing the Muslim world in the intellectual, cultural, political, media, economic and developmental fields and formulated a number of recommendations to effectively address them. On 7–8 December the Third Extraordinary Islamic Summit Conference met in Makkah. In his opening speech, the Saudi leader said:

> Islamic unity will not be achieved by bloodletting as the miscreants—in their misguided waywardness—insist on claiming. Fanaticism and extremism cannot grow on an earth whose soil is embedded in the spirit of tolerance, moderation, and balance.[10]

The Makkah summit of the OIC produced three main documents namely the Makkah Declaration, Ten-Year Programme of Action, and Eminent Persons' Report,[11] which lay down a comprehensive time-bound action plan to reform and restructure the OIC in order to enable it to overcome challenges facing the Muslim world concerning democracy, the defence of Islam, development, and projection of a soft image of Islam in the world.

'More than ever before', the Makkah Declaration stated, 'the Muslim world stands in dire need of a fresh vision to turn the tide' by renewing the 'loyalty of Muslims to true Islam' and playing 'an instrumental, proactive role in the service of humanity and human civilization'. While underscoring the fact that the Muslim world was 'too aware…of the internal and external threats that have helped to exacerbate (its) current plight, as they not only menace its very future but also that of the whole of humanity and civilization', the

Declaration rationalized OIC revitalization by foreseeing its natural culmination as 'a staunch counteraction of any miscreants who would wantonly work evil sedition, who would misguide and mislead, and would distort the loftiest tenets of our Islamic faith enshrined in its intrinsic call for love, peace, harmony, and the civilized way out'. The Declaration also highlighted the need for unity in the Muslim world, which requires Islamic scholars and experts of jurisprudence 'to unify their stand on exposing the corruption of these miscreants and the falsehood of their claims in a determined show of strength and undivided condemnation'.

After denouncing religious extremism within the world of Islam, the Declaration rejected terrorism in all its forms and manifestations, terming it 'a global phenomenon that is not confined to any particular religion, race, colour, or country'. Since terrorism can 'in no way be justified or rationalized,' the Declaration expressed the Muslim world's determination to develop 'national laws and legislations to criminalize every single terrorist practice and every single practice leading to the financing or instigation of terrorism', as well as to 'redouble and orchestrate international efforts to combat terrorism, including the establishment of an International Counter-Terrorism Centre', as endorsed by the International Conference on Combating Terrorism.

As part of the other two-policy documents approved at the Makkah summit, the OIC member states agreed to undertake a variety of measures to counter extremism and terrorism. In order to prevent a 'fringe' within the Muslim world from resorting to terrorism, the Muslim countries agreed,

> to persuade the big powers to address the root causes of terrorism and intensify coordination within OIC for combating terrorism; encourage interpretations of Islam which emphasize peace and non-violence and popularize principles or programmes which promote a balanced, contemporary, comprehensive and inclusive Islamic civilization and condemn the audacity of those who are not qualified in issuing religious rulings (*fatwa*), entrust the OIC Secretary General to invite a group from the members of the Islamic Fiqh Academy and eminent Islamic scholars from outside to prepare a detailed study to coordinate *fatwa* authorities in the Muslim world and counter religious and sectarian extremism.

In order to combat terrorism, the OIC was mandated to 'support efforts to develop an International Code of Conduct to Combat Terrorism' within the framework of the UN. Meanwhile, 'an observatory at the OIC General Secretariat will monitor all forms of Islamophobia, issue an annual report and ensure cooperation with the relevant governmental and non-government organizations to counter Islamophobia'. The OIC will also endeavour to 'have the UN adopt an international resolution to counter Islamophobia, and call upon all States to enact laws to counter it, including deterrent punishments'.

Linked to political challenges are some fundamental security issues confronting the Muslim world including conflict within and among Muslim nations, foreign occupation of Muslim lands, tensions arising from Muslim minority status in a number of countries and extremist tendencies due to feelings of injustice, hopelessness and desperation.

In the light of the above, the summit policy documents recommended the initiation of measures to overcome such security challenges. These included promoting Confidence-Building Measures (CBMs) and developing a system of Collective Security so that all Muslim countries could bind themselves together internationally to avoid border disputes and conflict, and reactivating the decision to establish an Islamic Court of Justice.

OIC member states also agreed to:

broadening the scope of Islamic education, with the aim of creating awareness about Islamic norms and teachings which oblige Muslims to practice the virtues of peace, moderation, tolerance, consultation, justice, freedom, equality and compassion; to seek knowledge and wisdom from all civilizations in the East and in the West; to respect the differences and promote peaceful interaction, cooperation and dialogue.

Besides including a number of other steps widening its scope, Islamic education will:

involve proper training of teachers and production of textbooks of Islamic religious education to prepare children for the challenges of religious pluralism, globalization, the knowledge-based economy, the revolution of Information Technology and the Moral Society.

Since the terrorist events of 11 September 2001, and in the wake of a number of terrorist attacks in the Muslim world before and after these events, the Muslim world leaders, particularly the Saudi leadership, have increasingly felt that there was an urgent need to restore the true image of Islam and Muslims in the world. Such a realization owes to two factors, one external and the other internal, namely the rise of Islamophobia in the West and the regressive projection of Islam by Muslim extremists. The Muslim leadership's perception appears to be that as long as the interpretation of Islam or Muslims remains predominantly in the hands of the extremists at home, or Western propagandists, the true image of Islam as a religion of peace, moderation and modernity will not be restored.[12] Unsurprisingly, therefore, the Makkah Summit documents repeatedly underscore the need for Muslim scholars and media to come forward and place their religion and the world in true and proper perspective. They include numerous references to the dangers of extremism and the urgency for moderation in the world of Islam. For the purpose, the Da'wa Department is assigned the additional task of tackling Islamophobia, even considering the option of referring it to the UN. An OIC think-tank is to be created and the Organization's media outfits are to be revamped. To snatch the initiative from the extremists with regard to the interpretation of what true Islam actually constitutes, or what

Jihad genuinely implies in a broader sense, the scope of the Islamic Fiqh Academy is to be broadened and Islamic education is to be brought in conformity with the universally practiced norms and values.[13]

There is also a growing perception among the Muslim leadership that the traditionally pursued, rhetoric-based confrontational approach has not paid any political dividends, and that the resort to such an approach in the post-9/11 world is unaffordable and potentially counter-productive. Consequently, the Summit policy documents depict an obvious preference on the part of the OIC to pursue a strategy of engagement with the Western world or non-Muslim powers of the East through a 'dialogue of civilizations'. In fact, the era of confrontational politics in the world of Islam seems to be largely over, as Muslim states become more realistic and pragmatic in their dealings with the Western world. The Muslim leadership's perception is that the OIC alone cannot accomplish its reformist agenda unless it cooperates with the Western world as well as regional and international organizations such as the United Nations and the European Union. For the purpose, the OIC has found willing partners in the UN and among Western governments and institutions. The Makkah Summit documents also emphasize the need for closer cooperation between the OIC and the UN and EU. In fact, since 2002, a UN Secretary-General-sponsored 'Alliance of Civilization' initiative has been under way between the OIC and the EU, led by Turkey on behalf of the former and Spain on behalf of the latter.[14] In

March 2008, King Abdullah bin Abdul Aziz also called for a dialogue among the three Abrahamic faiths of Islam, Christianity and Judaism, while arguing that the Kingdom's top clerics had given him approval to pursue this idea. For the purpose, the Saudi King said he planned to get the opinion of Muslim leaders from other countries.[15]

The very fact that the Muslim world is changing, as is clear from the recent moves for OIC reform and restructuring, and the practical instances of collective assertion by Muslim countries, is enough to envision an optimistic scenario for its future. All of this would not have come about if King Abdullah bin Abdul Aziz had not taken the lead in reforming the Muslim world body in response to challenges it is facing in the aftermath of the terrorist events of 11 September 2001, and terrorist attacks against Muslim countries themselves before and after these events. Had the Muslim leaders, particularly the Saudi leadership, been merely reacting to post-9/11 internal and external pressures, and consequently attempting to reform and restructure the OIC, the scope of the Muslim world's reform process and its outcome would have been limited and transitory in nature. However, it is not just the traditionally reactionary factor pushing the Muslim leaders to opt for change in the OIC. The impetus for this reform is largely indigenous which is an outcome of a growing realization on the part of Muslim leaders about the urgency of overcoming challenges pertaining to economic development, social progress, defence of Islam and the need to correct its distorted image in the world.

The above narration of the various steps that the Saudi government and its leadership have taken as part of the country's bilateral and multilateral diplomacy for countering terrorism make it quite obvious that the Kingdom has emerged as a pivotal international player when it comes to highlighting the threat of international terrorism and proposing short- and long-term global approaches for its viable resolution. Saudi Arabian strategy regarding terrorist financing, intelligence sharing, hunting down and exchange of terrorists in partnership with its global partners, the organization of the International Conference on Combating Terrorism, and the above-mentioned initiative to use the platform of the OIC to generate a collective Muslim world response to terrorism since it endangers Muslims and their religion, are all practical manifestations of the Saudi leadership's resolve to combat international terrorism through a proactive engagement of the world community.

Saudi Arabia is the citadel of Islam as it houses two of the holiest places of worship where, each year, millions of Muslims worship Almighty Allah and pay homage to the holy Prophet Muhammad (PBUH). Saudi Arabia stands for the unity of the Muslim *Ummah*. It is, therefore, no surprise that, whenever and wherever signs of disunity in the ranks of Muslim peoples surface, the Kingdom and its leadership have always attempted to mediate differences among their fellow Muslims—whether they were the Afghan *Mujahideen* groups on the eve of the withdrawal of Soviet troops from Afghanistan or, more recently, the rival Palestinian groups. Whether within the framework of the OIC, whose foundation is grounded in the Palestinian issue and which has always strived for the Palestinian cause, or on its own, Saudi Arabia has been in the forefront of the international campaign for achieving a just and fair settlement of the Palestinian issue which is one of the principal root causes of terrorism in the contemporary period. It is towards this end that King Abdullah bin Abdul Aziz had proposed a comprehensive peace plan which was also adopted by the March 2002 Arab League Summit.

The Saudi leadership's approach *vis-à-vis* all other regional conflicts in which Muslims have suffered, from Bosnia-Herzegovina and Chechnya in the 1990s to Iraq, Afghanistan and Kashmir at present, has been aimed at seeking their just and fair resolution through proactive bilateral and multilateral diplomacy. As said before, Saudi commitment against terrorism predates the terrorist events of 11 September 2001 and the consequent 'War on Terror'. By revoking the citizenship of Osama bin Laden, Saudi Arabia had acted wisely almost a decade before al-Qaeda conducted its deadliest-ever terrorist act in the United States. The Saudi leadership knew that the path some of those who had fought in the Afghan jihad against the Soviets had adopted was inhuman and un-Islamic.

Following the Soviet demise in Afghanistan, the intra-Afghan fighting began. Consequently, the Taliban emerged. Like Pakistan and the United Arab Emirates, Saudi Arabia recognized their regime, thinking they would bring peace to the war-torn nation. Instead, they made Afghanistan a sanctuary for al-Qaeda terrorism. The Taliban regime never heeded the Saudi advice for sanity and tolerance in their treatment of ethno-sectarian minorities, irresponsible conduct *vis-à-vis* the region and the world, and other deplorable acts such as the demolition of the Buddha statues. That the Taliban eventually had to pay a heavy price for all this was a foregone conclusion. Like all other nations in the Muslim world and elsewhere, Saudi Arabia is a well-wisher of the Afghan people and is doing whatever it can to help Afghanistan become stable, peaceful and prosperous.

THE INTERFAITH DIALOGUE

If the objective of peace in the world is to be achieved, it is absolutely essential that all religions learn to co-exist in harmony. The leaders of these religions together with heads of governments and states must demonstrate unequivocally their firm commitment to the cause of peace and they must endeavour to educate themselves in the virtues of tolerance and humaneness. For long they have stayed away from each other and for long have they been at loggerheads with each other. In the face of the threat posed by the demon of terrorism, it is vital that they come together on one platform as a reminder to the deviant minds that they stand united to confront them and shall, under no circumstances, succumb to their devilish machinations.

It is towards the fulfilment of this noble cause that the concept of the Interfaith Dialogue was initiated. It afforded a credible opportunity to leaders of all religions of the world to sit together and deliberate the causes of terrorism as well as the means to combat the scourge. The leaders of governments and states would also be part of this process of deliberations as their input would be critical and decisive in the formulation of a credible and sustaining strategy to fight and eliminate the heinous scourge of terrorism.

THE INTERFAITH DIALOGUE IN MAKKAH

The International Islamic Conference for Dialogue (IICFD), or Interfaith Dialogue, organized by the Muslim World Conference under the patronage of King Abdullah bin Abdul Aziz held in Makkah on 4–6 June 2008 is another pioneering initiative for bringing various religions of the world together with the intention of forging unity and harmony among them.[16]

The conference was held at a time when the world was faced with numerous challenges that pose a threat of mammoth proportions to humankind's future, and warn of further universal moral, social and environmental catastrophes as a result of disregard for the guidance of its Creator.

Inaugurating the conference, King Abdullah said that the participants were meeting to say to the whole world that they were a voice of justice and ethical human values, co-existence, judicious and wise dialogue and of exhortation and argument with what is best in compliance with the verse 'Invite (all) to the way of thy Lord with wisdom and beautiful preaching; and argue with them in ways that are best and most gracious'. (The holy Qur'an, 16:125)

King Abdullah emphasized the importance of dialogue in Islam and reminded the participants that the revealed messages have all called to the good of humankind, preserving human dignity and enhancing the values of ethics and truthfulness:

> We are commencing our dialogue with the confidence that we derive from our belief in God and with knowledge taken from the tolerance of religion, and that we debate in the best and the most gracious way. What we agree on, we hold fast onto and place in our hearts, and what we disagree on, we refer it to God saying to you be your way and to me mine.

The participants discussed four broad issues including Islamic legitimacy for dialogue, methodology, rules, regulations and means of dialogue, whom to engage in dialogue and the basis and themes of dialogue.[17]

After a thorough review of the challenges that face humanity, the conference issued a declaration for all governments, organizations and people irrespective of their religions and cultures and called on them to undertake steps to foster understanding that we believe in God as the creator, worship Him alone and seek guidance that He revealed to His prophets and messengers, challenge injustice, tyranny, despotism and hegemony, help each other in ending wars, conflicts and international problems, and work together for the promotion of a culture of tolerance and dialogue.[18]

The conference also called for cooperation with each other for the promotion of moral values and the building of international ethical arrangements that resist the attack of moral deviation and provide solutions for the dangers surrounding the family in a manner that secures the right of all to live within a happy family unit. It urged for working together as inhabitants of earth according to the wish of God who authorized our father Adam and his progeny to reform the earth and halt aggression on the right of the coming generations. The conference also called for cooperation among the world community in eliminating corruption and unhappiness, which need to be remedied through the mercy of God that is the essence of the message sent to the Prophet Muhammad (PBUH): 'We sent thee not but as a mercy for all creatures'. (The holy Qur'an, 21:107)

THE INTERFAITH DIALOGUE IN MADRID

The conference in Makkah was followed by another conference in Madrid, Spain on 16–18 July 2008. The participants, representing all major religions and cultures of the world, considered dialogue as the best way for mutual understanding and cooperation in human relations as well as for peaceful co-existence among nations.

In this context, the participants affirmed the principles[19] of the unity of humankind in the original creation and equality among human beings irrespective of their colour, ethnic background and culture, purity of the nature of human beings as they were created: liking good and disliking evil and inclined to justice and avoiding injustice. Such nature leads human beings to show mercy and seek certainty and belief.

Diversity of cultures and civilizations among people is a sign of God and a cause for human advancement and prosperity. The heavenly messages aim at realizing the obedience of people to their Creator and achieving happiness, justice, security and peace for humankind. These messages call for spreading virtue through wisdom and politeness, and rejecting extremism and terrorism.

The participants also urged for respecting heavenly religions, condemning any insults to their symbols, combating the exploitation of religion and the instigation of racial discrimination, observing peace, honouring agreements and respecting the unique traditions of all peoples and their right to security, freedom and self-determination which are the basis for building good relations among all people. Achieving this is a major objective of all religions and prominent cultures.

The participants noted that dialogue is one of the essentials of life. It is also one of the most important means for knowing each other, mutual cooperation, exchange of interests and realizing the truth, which contributes to the happiness of humankind.

After thoroughly reviewing the process of dialogue, the conference noted that terrorism was one of the most serious obstacles confronting dialogue and co-existence. It was a universal phenomenon, which required unified international effort to combat it in a serious, responsible and just manner. This demands an international agreement on defining terrorism, addressing its root causes and achieving justice and stability in the world.

With the intention of achieving the above, the conference adopted recommendations[20] rejecting theories that call for the clash of civilizations and cultures, and warned of the dangers of campaigns seeking to deepen conflicts and destabilizing peace and security. The conference also called for enhancing common human values, cooperating in their dissemination within societies and solving the problems that hinder their achievement. It urged the dissemination of a culture of tolerance and understanding through dialogue so as to become a framework for international relations through holding conferences and symposia as well as developing relevant cultural, educational and media programmes. It underscored the need for agreeing on international guidelines for dialogue among the followers of religions and cultures so as to strengthen stability and achieve prosperity for all humans. It urged governmental and non-governmental organizations to issue a document that stipulates respect for religions and their symbols, prohibition of their denigration and the repudiation of those who commit such acts.

In order to fulfil the desired objectives of dialogue, the participants of the conference agreed to form a working team to study the problems hindering dialogue and preventing it from realizing its desired results, enhance cooperation among religious, cultural, educational and media establishments to deepen and consolidate ethical values, encourage noble social practices, organize inter-religious and inter-cultural meetings, conduct research, execute media programmes and use the Internet and other media for dissemination of a culture of peace, understanding and co-existence.[21] The participants also agreed to work for promoting the issue of dialogue among the followers of religions, civilizations and cultures within the youth, cultural, educational and media activities, and called upon the United Nations General Assembly to support the results recommended by this conference.

It was strongly proposed to make use of the recommendations of the conference to enhance the process of dialogue among the followers of religions, civilizations and cultures through organizing a special UN session on dialogue.

THE INTERFAITH DIALOGUE IN NEW YORK

Upon the initiative of King Abdullah bin Abdul Aziz, the General Assembly convened a plenary high-level meeting during its 63rd session held in New York on 12–13 November 2008.

Taking note of the initiative of the King of Saudi Arabia and the International Conference on Interfaith Dialogue held in Madrid, Spain from 16 to 18 July 2008 that was hosted by the King and the government of Spain, the General Assembly reiterated its call for promoting a culture of tolerance and mutual understanding through dialogue and supporting the initiatives of religious leaders, civil society and states seeking to entrench a culture of peace, understanding, tolerance and respect for human rights among the proponents of various faiths, cultures and civilizations.

The text of the final communiqué,[22] as mentioned below, underlines the importance of the interfaith dialogue and the contribution it can make in securing peace in the world:

The meeting reiterated the goals and principles contained in the UN Charter and the International Declaration of Human Rights. It recalled the commitment of all countries, under the UN Charter, to encourage the respect for human rights and basic liberties for all which include freedom of belief and expression without any discrimination on the basis of ethnicity, nationality, language or religion. The participating countries voiced their concern over the growing cases of bigotry, prejudice, hate spreading and persecution of religious minorities. They stressed on the importance of encouraging dialogue, understanding, tolerance among the people and respect for their religions, cultures and different beliefs.

The participating countries also reaffirmed their denunciation of using religion as justification for killing innocent people, terrorist practices, violence and coercion which are unmistakably contradictory to the call of all religions for peace, justice and equality. The General Assembly took note of the initiative of the King of Saudi Arabia and the holding of the International Conference on Interfaith Dialogue in Madrid, Spain from 16 to 18 July 2008. It restated its call for promoting the culture of tolerance, mutual understanding through dialogue and supporting the initiatives of religions, civil society leaders and heads of states for deepening the culture of peace, understanding, tolerance and respect for human rights among the followers of different religions, cultures and civilizations. The participating countries expressed their resolve for shoring up and strengthening the existing bodies of the United Nations for the promotion of tolerance, human rights, protection of family, environment, broadening education, elimination of poverty, drugs, crime, terrorism and taking into account the positive contribution of religions, beliefs, human and moral values for meeting these challenges.

The recommendations contained in the three Interfaith conferences held in Makkah, Madrid, and New York are, indeed, epoch making initiatives that would open a new leaf in the chequered history of the world. These are milestones that would unfurl the dawn of hope and peace for the people of the followers of various religions and cultures and lead to elimination of conflicts and confrontation. These recommendations would also provide a stable and sustaining basis for forging unity among the peoples of the world irrespective of their religious, cultural, ethnic, social, or any other affiliations.

NOTES

1. *Saudi Arabia and the Fight against Terrorist Financing*, op. cit.
2. See, *Initiatives and Actions Taken by the Kingdom of Saudi Arabia in the War on Terrorism*, op. cit.
3. *Saudi Arabia and the Fight against Terrorist Financing*, op. cit.
4. For a list of people extradited from and to Saudi Arabia, see, *Initiatives and Actions Taken by the Kingdom of Saudi Arabia in the War on Terrorism*, op. cit.
5. Cordesman, op. cit.

6. See, *Initiatives and Actions Taken by the Kingdom of Saudi Arabia in the War on Terrorism*, op. cit.

7. See, the speech at the official website of the Ministry of Foreign Affairs, Kingdom of Saudi Arabia, http://www.mofa.gov.sa/detail.asp?InServiceID=205&intemplatekey=MainPage, accessed on 15 May 2008.

8. Ibid.

9. For OIC's proactive role in recent years, see Ishtiaq Ahmad 'The Organization of Islamic Conference: From Ceremonial Politics to Politicization?,' in Harders & Legrenzi, eds., *Beyond Regionalism? Regional Cooperation, Regionalism and Regionalisation in the Middle East* (London: Ashgate, 2008).

10. See the speech at official website of the OIC, http://www.oic-oci.org/ex-summit/english/speeches/king-speech-sum.htm, accessed on 15 May 2008.

11. Makkah Summit documents are available at official website of the OIC, http://www.oic-oci.org/ex-summit/english/, accessed on 15 May 2008.

12. Karima Rhanem, 'Challenges Facing OIC Summit,' *Morocco Times*, 12 December 2005; 'OIC Summit to Seek Moderate Islam Image after Terror Attacks,' *AFP*, 5 December 2005.

13. Makkah Summit documents, op. cit.

14. United Nations, 'Alliance of Civilizations'. Available from http://www.unaoc.org/, accessed on 15 May 2006.

15. Richard Owen, 'Saudi King Calls for Interfaith Talks', *Time Magazine*, 25 March 2008.

16. *The International Islamic Conference for Interfaith Dialogue,* organized by The Muslim World League, Makkah, 4–6 June 2008.

17. Ibid.

18. Ibid.

19. *The Madrid Declaration: The World Conference on Dialogue,* organized by The Muslim World League, Madrid, Spain, 13–15 July 2008.

20. Ibid.

21. Ibid.

22. For the text of the Final Communiqué of the Interfaith Conference in New York, see Internal Circular, Government of Saudi Arabia, 15 November 2008.

7

Emulating Saudi Strategy:
Some Examples

The discussion in the previous two chapters makes it clear that Saudi Arabia has pursued a comprehensive approach to combating terrorism at home and abroad—an approach that has succeeded. Accordingly, Saudi Arabia's comprehensive strategy to combat international terrorism has won the Kingdom an increasing level of global acknowledgement. Not just that, from Indonesia to Egypt to Iraq, more and more Muslim countries have started to adopt the Saudi model to combat terrorism. The Kingdom's counter-terrorism approach has become a role model for other Muslim countries that are faced with the terrorist threat but have been unable to combat it successfully. The success of the Saudi counter-terrorism policy is visible on the ground, as the Kingdom has not seen a repeat of terrorism activities such as the two terrorist attacks in 2003.

It is important to learn how other Muslim countries are trying to emulate the Saudi experience in counter-terrorism. For the purpose, the cases of Egypt and Iraq will be discussed briefly, as they are still at a relatively initial stage of the experiment, while the case of Indonesia will be discussed in some detail since its 'soft approach' to tackling terrorism is quite similar to that of Saudi Arabia and, like Saudi Arabia, this has produced credible results. However, it must be mentioned that, in addition to emulating the success stories of Muslim countries like Saudi Arabia, each country of the Muslim world currently engaged in counter-extremism and counter-terrorism campaigns, has to adopt additional measures, since the circumstances and challenges *vis-à-vis* the extremism and terrorism it faces may drastically differ from the problems confronted by counter-terrorism's success stories like Saudi Arabia. Afghanistan may be a pertinent example in this context because it is a country that has seen recurrent phases of a variety of warfare over several decades.

What is critically important is to understand that, alongside incorporating general features from the successful Saudi counter-terrorism strategy, each country will have to add an indigenous flavour for it to work successfully in its respective environment. In other words, for any strategy to work effectively, efficiently and successfully in any country, the stress should be on making it a home grown operation.

THE CASE OF INDONESIA

In the aftermath of the terrorist events of 11 September 2001 in the United States, Indonesia became an active US partner in the international campaign against al-Qaeda-inspired terrorism only a couple of years after the 2002 terrorist bombings in Bali and subsequent terrorist events in the country and across South-East Asia, making this region the

Second Front in the 'War on Terror'. As a result of the measures adopted by the Indonesian government under President Susilo Bambang Yudhoyono, terrorism practiced by the al-Qaeda-linked Jemaah Islamiyah in the country has waned, making Indonesia one of the world's most successful models of counter-terrorism.[1]

The story of how al-Qaeda came into being in the immediate aftermath of the end of the Afghan–Arab jihad against Soviet troops in Afghanistan has been frequently narrated. We are also generally aware of the circumstances that led al-Qaeda's founding leader, Osama bin Laden, to declare international jihad against the United States and its allies, civilian as well as military, from al-Qaeda sanctuaries in Taliban-led Afghanistan. The fallout from the Afghan jihad was not just visible in Afghanistan, especially in the shape of the Taliban's capture of power in the country, but also in other regions. Despite the fact that Indonesia, the world's largest Muslim country located in South-East Asia, was geographically far apart from Afghanistan and from the direct reach of al-Qaeda, the terrorist organization was able to threaten the peace and stability of Indonesia in particular, and the South-East Asian region in general, through its local affiliates such as Indonesia's Jemaah Islamiyah and the Abu Sayyaf group in the Philippines.[2]

In Indonesia's case, Jemaah Islamiyah took advantage of the country's political turbulence and economic meltdown in the late 1990s to build terror cells and promote radical Islam across the archipelago. Historically, Indonesians subscribed to a tolerant religious creed, but Jemaah Islamiyah and other deviant groups began to strike at these local traditions. They began to set up networks of boarding schools across the country to attract young men away from the under-funded public system. Jemaah Islamiyah's charismatic leader, Abu Bakar Baasyir, travelled throughout Indonesia preaching violent jihad. With a growing pool of potential recruits, Jemaah Islamiyah expanded and started mounting increasingly sophisticated terror operations. For instance, on Christmas Eve in 2000, it orchestrated the bombing of over thirty churches, killing eighteen people.[3] Jemaah Islamiyah's terrorism was not confined to Indonesia. The group was also cooperating closely with its counterparts in the region including Abu Sayyaf and other deviant outfits in Malaysia and Thailand, which, like the Philippines and Indonesia, witnessed a series of terrorist events.

By the time al-Qaeda orchestrated the terrorist attacks of 11 September 2001, radicalism had taken firm root in South-East Asia with Indonesia and the Philippines being its principal targets. The Indonesian government of Presidents Abdurrahman Wahid and Megawati Sukarnoputri and President Gloria Arroyo's regime in the Philippines did not fully recognize the danger. Indonesia's Vice President Hamzah Haz, actually celebrated the 9/11 attacks, announcing his hope that the deaths of 3,000 people in the World Trade Centre would help 'cleanse America of its sins'.[4] In 2002, he reportedly had dinner with several Islamic radical leaders, including Abu Bakar Baasyir, and announced there were no terrorists in Indonesia. The same year, in front of a cheering parliament, outgoing President Sukarnoputri demanded that the United States should not bomb Afghanistan during the month of Ramadan. Indonesian authorities also failed to prevent a radical outfit, Darul Islam, from recruiting 300 volunteers to fight against the Americans in Afghanistan.[5]

Then, on the fateful day of 12 October 2002, Jemaah Islamiyah terrorists set off two powerful bombs on the Indonesian island of Bali. Detonated in the heart of the tourist district, they blew up two popular bars, killing 202 people—visiting Australians, Americans, and other foreign nationals, as well as Indonesians—and wounding still more. It was the worst terrorist attack in the country's history. In 2003, Jemaah Islamiyah struck at the heart of Indonesian power, bombing a Marriott hotel in the Jakarta neighbourhood that is home to the country's most important banks, oil companies, and other economic players. Soon after, militants bombed the Australian embassy. Despite these audacious attacks by Islamic radicals belonging to Jemaah Islamiyah, the government of President Sukarnoputri failed to comprehend the terrorist threat to Indonesia, and, therefore, did not opt for any credible counter-terrorism strategy,[6] especially in partnership with Western powers such as Australia and the United States.

It was only with the coming to power of Susilo Bambang Yudhoyono as President in 2004, that the Indonesian government started to take the challenge of terrorism with the seriousness it deserved. The counter-terrorism strategy that has resulted from President Yudhoyono's firm political resolve and deep personal conviction to fight terrorism has made a credible difference in Indonesia. Under his leadership, Indonesia has transformed itself from a country riddled with deviant religious movements and terror threats to one of the world's few triumphs in fighting terrorism. Even better, Jakarta has succeeded without resorting to the draconian anti-terror tactics increasingly preferred by governments fighting terrorism, from the United States and Iraq to Afghanistan and other countries. Jemaah Islamiyah is now struggling to survive. With assistance from the United States, Australia, Malaysia and the Philippines, President Yudhoyono's government tracked the Bali bombers and other Jemaah Islamiyah members. Elsewhere in the region, governments have shown similar commitment. Consequently, like Jemaah Islamiyah, Abu Sayyaf's ability to commit terrorism is now severely restricted. Across South-East Asia, terrorism has significantly weakened, as the region's leaders openly wage war on terror. Moreover, the United States has played a leading role in these successes, and it has done so without creating much in the way of an anti-American reaction. Indeed, South East Asia is proving to be a model for the 'long war' against terror.

Indonesia under President Yudhoyono has followed a 'soft approach' against terrorism. This approach is based upon a four-pronged strategy including:

1. Making counter-terrorism a genuinely national campaign;
2. Enlisting former terrorists in the counter-terrorism campaign;
3. Letting the elite police, rather than the army, lead the fight against terrorists, and
4. Prosecuting terrorists judiciously and transparently.

MAKING THE 'WAR ON TERROR' AS INDONESIA'S OWN

This is perhaps the most important element of Indonesia's counter-extremism and counter-terrorism strategy. While pursuing counter-terrorism policies, the Indonesian government has made sure that these policies should be perceived publicly as part of a local or national fight, rather than something imposed upon the country's leadership by the United States or the Western world. Soon after his election as President in 2004, Mr Yudhoyono made a public declaration of war on terrorism and vowed to convince his countrymen that religious radicalism was a threat not just to the West, but to Indonesians themselves.[7] His government has closely worked with the United States in counter-terrorism, yet, in domestic public perceptions, this fight has gone down as Indonesia's own. For its part, the US policy has also been to let the Indonesian government stand on its own. In providing military assistance to Indonesia, Washington has chosen wisely to play a behind-the-scenes role, dispatching advisers, communications technology, and weaponry rather than taking the point position itself.

The United States has eschewed the kind of inflammatory rhetoric that could allow terrorists to cast their fight as a struggle against a foreign crusader. That is why the Indonesian leadership has been able to avoid charges of becoming American stooges. Beyond helping to track and kill terrorists, Washington has promoted economic development in the region and has tried to assist in settling local conflicts that, very often, have taken on an Islamic cast. The Yudhoyono regime has also worked closely with regional governments, especially the Philippines, Thailand and Malaysia, mostly within the framework of the Association of South-East Asian Nations (ASEAN) to capture terror suspects and share intelligence to pre-empt terrorist events. A Joint Counter-Terrorism Centre now exists in Malaysia. ASEAN members have also tightened their laws on money laundering—a key source of terrorist finance.[8] All of this has made counter-terrorism either a national or a regional fight, and not a struggle being waged on behalf of the United States or the Western world.

ENLISTING FORMER TERRORISTS TO CAMPAIGN AGAINST TERRORISM

A second, but equally important, element of the Indonesian model, essentially based on the Saudi counter-terrorism experience, is the recognition that the words of militants matter more to other potential militants[9]—say, young men thinking of joining a terror group—than some sermon from Muslim moderates. President Yudhoyono has proved to be a strong voice for secularism, thus weakening the appeal of Muslim radicals. In order to emphasize the seriousness of the threat, his government has televised the videos of local suicide bombers and has recruited top Muslim clerics to issue public messages against the terrorists. Jakarta has even employed former terrorists to preach that violence has no place in Islam.

As stated before, Saudi Arabia has also practiced the same approach aimed at building up an extensive web of former militants working to persuade hardliners to change sides. The Indonesian government co-opts those among the terrorists, suspected or convicted of terrorism, who show a commitment to help authorities and express regret for their terrorist actions. In engaging the terrorists, Indonesian authorities often exploit a long-standing rift in the militant movement over the morality and strategic benefit of bombing soft targets such as the Bali nightclubs. Those cooperating with authorities can expect shorter sentences, cash payments, and medical care for themselves or relatives. A few work publicly with authorities. One former Jemaah Islamiyah regional leader, a Malaysian named Nasir Abbas, occasionally briefs the media alongside the police. Most remain behind the scenes, identifying a voice recording or photo of a suspect or meeting detainees in jail to challenge their views. The strategy has paid dividends.[10]

LETTING THE ELITE POLICE LEAD THE FIGHT AGAINST TERRORISTS

Thirdly, the Indonesia model relies upon effective police work rather than military force. President Yudhoyono seems to understand that, in many developing nations, the military is not the best institution to tackle terror. Instead of relying on the armed forces, elements of which have a reputation for corruption and repression, the Indonesian government created an elite counter-terrorism police force called Detachment 88, a 300-man elite counter-terrorism special contingent that is trained to counter various terrorist threats and assist regular police officers in investigations. Trained and equipped by the United States, Detachment 88 has taken the lead in fighting Jemaah Islamiyah[11] and has helped capture hundreds of terror suspects and seize caches of weapons, explosives and chemicals in numerous raids in Central and East Java.

For instance, in November 2005, the elite force succeeded in killing Azahari bin Hussain, a Malaysian national accused of masterminding the recruiting and training of Jemaah Islamiyah's suicide bombers. In June 2006, it captured Abu Dujana, the head of Jemaah Islamiyah's military wing, and another of the group's supreme commander Zarkasih. This was the first time the government arrested top Jemaah Islamiyah terrorists and managed to have them disclose valuable information on the group's structure, cells, past operations and future plans, including Abu Bakar Baasyir's role in the Bali bombings.[12]

Prosecuting Terrorists Judiciously and Transparently

A fourth element in Indonesia's 'soft approach' against alleged terrorists is a fair trial. Rather than tossing terrorism suspects in jails indefinitely, or torturing them, President Yudhoyono's government has prosecuted cases against terror suspects in courts in open trials, which has helped keep public opinion in favour of the government.[13]

Under the new leadership, not only are the security forces unable to take extra-judicial steps against terror suspects, the terror trials are also disposed off judicially. Detachment 88 has succeeded through dogged investigative work, and not by resorting to brutal interrogation techniques. The Yudhoyono government has expanded its fight against terror while, at the same time, instituting democratic reforms, establishing national human rights bodies, and generally creating a more open, accountable government.[14] No surprise that Jakarta's counter-terrorism efforts continue to have a high standing in public opinion.

OTHER CASES IN THE MUSLIM WORLD

Like Saudi Arabia, the Egyptian government is engaged in an extensive de-radicalization programme that has worked, as no terrorist instance of the scale of the November 1997 massacre of sixty-two foreign tourists in Luxor has occurred so far. Under the de-radicalization programme, the detainees serving sentences on charges of inciting, or undertaking terrorism, are allowed by Egyptian authorities to meet and consult each other in prison and hold dialogue with clerics from Al-Azhar University which is recognized as one of the leading authorities on Islamic jurisprudence in the Muslim world. The programme has successfully converted and rehabilitated members of the Gama'a Islamiyya, once the largest deviant organization in the Arab world, which mounted countless armed attacks starting in the 1980s until agreeing to a ceasefire with the Egyptian government after the Luxor massacre. The Islamic group's top ideologues, who are now mostly freed, have written 25 volumes of revisions in a series called *Tashih al-Mafahim* (Corrections of Concepts), addressing key doctrinal issues such as the concept of *Takfir*— declaring a Muslim an apostate, and therefore, permissible to be killed, attacks on civilians and foreign tourists, and waging jihad against a Muslim ruler who does not apply Shariah law.[15]

Perhaps the biggest success of the Egyptian de-radicalization programme, thus far, is the recantation of radicalism by Dr Fadl, also known as Sayyid Imam Abdulaziz al-Sharif, who is the founding leader of the Egyptian Al-Jihad Organization and a former compatriot of al-Qaeda ideologue Dr Ayman Al-Zawahiri. In May 2007, *Asharq Al-Awsat,* one of the Arab world's leading newspapers, published a letter by Dr Fadl, in which he issued a call urging all 'jihadists' and their movements in the world to ensure that their 'jihadist' operations are carried out in accordance with the rules of Shariah. He stressed that his call was necessary at present because of the rise in new forms of un-Islamic fighting and killing in the name of jihad that violate Shariah law, like the killing of people based on their nationality, skin or hair colour, or for being affiliated with a certain sect, and also the killing of innocent Muslims or non-Muslims. In the letter, Dr Fadl urged 'jihadists' not to use the excuse of human shields to expand the circle of killing, and to refrain from stealing and destroying property, as all these actions constitute aggression. Almighty God, he explained, prohibits aggression during jihad as illustrated by the Qur'anic injunction: 'Fight in the cause of God those who fight you, but do not transgress the limits; for God loveth not transgressors'.[16]

Dr Fadl is serving a life sentence in Egypt in connection with a 1999 terrorist case, in which members of Al-Jihad had unsuccessfully attempted to blow-up the Egyptian embassy in Albania. Although Fadl had never set foot in Albania, many of those arrested there had identified Fadl as the past Emir of the group. It is generally believed that Dr Fadl has repented and recanted his previously held notions of violent jihad as a result of a long process of reflection and debate, facilitated by the Egyptian government's de-radicalization programme. Dr Fadl had authored the most important book on 'jihadist' jurisprudence in the past quarter century, *The Basic Principles in Making Preparations for Jihad*. This book is considered as the 'jihadist' movements' constitution, laying down the rules of jurisprudence for combat operations by 'jihadist' groups, including al-Qaeda. After recanting his previous thoughts, Dr Fadl has authored a new 100-page book, *Advice Regarding the*

Conduct of Jihadist Action in Egypt and the World, which he said was not addressed to any particular group and does not criticize any particular party. It is a collection of rules to help jihadists avoid violating Shariah during their conduct of jihad. From November 2007, the Egyptian daily *Al-Masry Al-Yom* began serializing the new book by Dr Fadl.[17]

From the already published sections of the book, it is apparent that Dr Fadl is reinterpreting the meaning of jihad in ways that explicitly forbid declarations of *Takfir* (under most circumstances) and the killing of non-Muslims in Muslim countries or members of other Muslim sects. Dr Fadl now rejects the 'jihad-centric' view of Islam characteristic of 'Salafi–Jihadist' doctrine, while demanding that jihad be understood within a more rigorous understanding of Shariah and jurisprudence, and specifically refutes a range of interpretations of jihad which have justified attacks on state employees and government officials, civilians, tourists, Shias, and non-Muslims in Muslim countries or in their own countries. On the proliferation of proclamations of *Takfir*, Dr Fadl's revised text declares that this should be a legal (Shariah) judgement, not a political or intellectual accusation—as with jihad, seeking to establish rules to govern it rather than to reject it.[18]

The Egyptian success against deviant thought and practice is significantly important, as the roots of the al-Qaeda movement are located in the peculiar Egyptian socio-political experience in the past half a century and more. The Muslim Brotherhood and its affiliates initially targeted the Egyptian state. It is only due to some international developments, including the Israeli occupation of Palestine and the Soviet occupation of Afghanistan, that the leaders and followers of such deviant organizations were able to spread their tentacles to the wider Middle East or South-West Asia. Obviously, a reversal of such movements grounded in the philosophy of a distorted version of global jihad requires that sources of conflicts in the Muslim world such as Palestine must be resolved urgently. However, in so far as the jihad against the Soviets was concerned, that is an old story. What followed afterwards in Afghanistan has largely been a Muslim-fighting-fellow-Muslim story.

Ending the war on Afghanistan or the Israeli occupation of Palestine is, and should be, the Muslim world's top priority. However, the key question is whether this noble objective should be achieved peacefully or through violent means, including the use of terror. Given Islam's inherent pacifist creed, highlighted amply on the foregoing pages, the Muslim world has no choice but to cater for a peaceful resolution of all its disputes, within the Muslim world or with non-Muslim states. There is no rational, moral, or religious ground for doing otherwise. It is in this broader context that the importance of the Egyptian government's de-radicalization programme premised on the Saudi initiative for the purpose should be understood. A country from where deviant thoughts and movements have significantly generated has to take the lead in reversing deviant tendencies and activities within its domain to put the genie of violent jihad, grounded in the utter distortion of the fundamentals of Islam, back in the bottle.

Like Egypt, the contours of the Saudi counter-terrorism strategy are also increasingly visible in Iraq, where al-Qaeda has tried to benefit from the precarious security environment since the arrival of the US-led coalition forces in the country in March 2003. Over time, the al-Qaeda leadership leasing suicide-bombing missions in Iraq seemed to succeed in its terrorist mission, as terrorist attacks against Iraqi government officials and security personnel, US-led coalition forces, and against the various ethnic and sectarian communities of the country, including both Sunnis and Shias, gained momentum. To counter that, the Iraqi government and coalition authorities have, in recent months, attempted to steal the initiative from al-Qaeda by isolating the terror network from the general Iraqi population aggrieved due to the post-March 2003 deterioration in the country's security environment characterized by a horrific killing spree with Iraqi people as its foremost victims.

Elsewhere in the Muslim world, the leadership of the countries afflicted by terrorist violence, from Afghanistan to Pakistan, have started realizing the importance of practicing a comprehensive counter-terrorism approach, inclusive of both military and non-military means, but preferring the latter to the former. This is the only way we can find a long lasting solution to the problem of terrorism, and this has precisely been the Saudi way of countering the threat of terrorism in all of its forms and manifestations.

PAKISTAN AND SAUDI ANTI-TERRORISM MODEL

The religious, tribal, cultural, and social similarities between Saudi Arabia and Pakistan make the latter an ideal country to look towards the Saudi model for guidance. The vast upsurge of violence in Pakistan ever since the US-led incursion into neighbouring Afghanistan has bedevilled Pakistani policy makers in their pursuit to find a credible solution to solve the crisis. The ever-growing pressure from the international community, led by the United States of America, to 'do more' to uproot the scourge of terrorism has worsened matters for the government in Pakistan.

For Pakistan, there is a lot to learn from the Saudi counter-terrorism model, or, for that matter, that of Indonesia. As the preceding discussion suggests, it is only when the leaderships of the two countries fully understood the gravity of the indigenous terrorist threat and its manifold repercussions and finally concluded that combating this threat was an urgent national obligation, that credible success against terrorism was realized.

In Pakistan's case, the gruesome events of recent years have established beyond any doubt that religiously motivated terrorism poses the most potent danger to the people and the state. Perhaps that is why its leadership has also started perceiving the war against terrorism, first and foremost, as Pakistan's own war, which has to be fought with all possible indigenous means in cooperation with the international community.

As soon as the Prime Minister of Pakistan took over, he declared the 'War on Terror' as his foremost priority; adding that peace talks and aid programmes would be more effective than weapons in fighting terrorism. Pakistani tribal areas have long suffered from backwardness. There is a dire need for comprehensive economic, social, and political reforms because poverty and illiteracy are promoting terrorism. 'We are ready to talk to all those people who give up arms and are ready to embrace peace', the Prime Minister of Pakistan said in his first major speech before the National Assembly in March 2008.[19]

This comprehensive approach should include a host of economic and political initiatives and give less importance to solving a complex problem such as terrorism through the use of military force alone. Pakistan's counter-terrorism and counter-extremism policy should place a greater emphasis on political, educational, and economic initiatives and less on the military operations.

What may also be of critical relevance in the launch of this counter-terrorism strategy, that lays equal emphasis on adopting measures other than the use of force alone, include the availability of funds for sustaining such an initiative. That is where the understanding, support, and help of the international community would play a pivotal role and would, in actual effect, determine the success or otherwise of any such initiative. These remedial measures should be focused on the needs of education, health, population welfare, medical care, provision of jobs for elimination of poverty and other allied projects.

Obviously, if the pro-Taliban elements continue to use the tribal areas of Pakistan as a sanctuary for conducting insurgent operations into Afghanistan against NATO-led forces, then even the government will be forced to allow the option of military operations. However, if the preference in the counter-terrorism and counter-extremism policy is for political and economic initiatives, then the pro-Taliban forces in the tribal areas will have no justification for engaging in cross-border insurgency in Afghanistan. A democratic regime always has a range of options available to solve a highly complex problem, which terrorism is. For doing so, however, it needs the help of the international community, particularly in the economic and political fields. Terrorism does not have only a security dimension. Therefore, it cannot be combated through military operations alone. It requires a multi-faceted and multi-dimensional strategy. Saudi Arabia could share the ingredients of such a strategy with Pakistan in terms of lessons it has learnt while achieving success against terrorism in the country in the security, financial, and educational domains.

THE 'WAR ON TERROR' IN AFGHANISTAN

In so far as the 'War on Terror' in Afghanistan is concerned, one of the reasons why it has failed to make a difference on the ground despite the passage of so many years is because the use of force as a necessary immediate security requirement has not been accompanied by a credible multi-faceted, long term strategy of rooting out the sources of deviant religious behaviour and its terrorist manifestation. The UN Mission for Afghanistan (UNAMA) may have supervised a democratic political process and International Security Assistance Forces (ISAF) led by NATO may have sponsored reformation of the security apparatus, undertaken reconstruction and counter-narcotics initiatives or supervised disarmament, demobilization and rehabilitation programmes, in addition to performing its principal security role. But, the situation in Afghanistan continues to deteriorate, as a large majority of Afghan people remain beyond the reach of UNAMA or ISAF-led reformation initiatives. There are also a host of political grievances revolving around ethno-nationalist factors. There is hardly any effective governmental initiative in sight that aims to win the hearts and minds campaign, to dissuade the deviants from obscurantist behaviour and disengage them from acts of terrorism. The problem is likely to conflagrate in the absence of a strategy that prefers a non-military solution to a military solution. The need is to adopt a creative, long-term path to root out problems regarding this complex issue.

The Saudi model remains a priority consideration in view of a vast similarity of problems and environments that exist in most of the Muslim countries. Its effectiveness and comprehensiveness are both reasons to pursue it for combating the curse of terrorism in all its manifestations and, ultimately, lead the way to a world free of the threat of terror.

NOTES

1. For a comprehensive analysis of Indonesia's counter-terrorism strategy, see Ishtiaq Ahmad, 'Indonesia's Counter-Terrorism Success: Lessons for Pakistan's Fight against Terrorism,' paper presented at International Seminar on Enhancing Pakistan–Indonesia Relations: Perspectives and Challenges, Area Study Centre for Far East and Southeast Asia (Jamshoro, Pakistan: University of Sindh, 18 November 2007).

2. Maria Ressa, *Seeds of Terror: An Eyewitness Account of Al-Qaeda's Newest Center of Operations in Southeast Asia* (New York: Free Press, 2003). Ahmad, ibid.

3. Joshua Kurlantzick, 'Where the War on Terror is Succeeding,' *Commentary* (Carnegie Endowment for International Peace, May 2007), ibid.

4. Ibid.

5. Dana R. Dillon, 'Make Fighting Terrorism the First Priority,' *The Asian Wall Street Journal*, 20 October 2004. Ahmad, ibid.

6. Kurlantzick, 'Where the War on Terror is Succeeding,' op. cit.

7. Joshua Kurlantzick, 'How Indonesia is Winning its War on Terror,' *Time Magazine*, 9 August 2007. Ahmad, op. cit.

8. Kurlantzick, 'Where the War on Terror is Succeeding,' op. cit.

9. Kurlantzick, 'How Indonesia is Winning its War on Terror,' op. cit.

10. Chris Brummitt, 'South-East Asia Beats Back Al-Qaeda', *The Associated Press*, 10 October 2007.

11. Kurlantzick, 'How Indonesia is Winning its War on Terror,' op. cit.

12. Abdullah Al Madani, 'Indonesia's Success in Its War on Terror,' *Gulf News*, 1 July 2007.

13. Kurlantzick, 'How Indonesia is Winning Its War on Terror,' op. cit.

14. Ibid.

15. Ishtiaq Ahmad, 'Repenting and Recanting Religious Raduicalism,' *Weekly Pulse*, 23–29 May 2008.

16. Mohammed Al Shafey, 'Egypt: Jailed Al-Qaeda Ideologue Urges Halt to Attacks Contradicting Islamic Law Asharq Al-Awsat,' 8 May 2007.

Available from http://aawsat.com/english/news.asp?section=1&id=8894, accessed on 20 May 2008.

17. Jailan Halawi, 'Bidding Violence Farewell,' *Al-Ahram Weekly*, 22–28 November 2007. Available from http://weekly.ahram.org.eg/2007/872/eg5.htm, accessed on 20 May 2008.

18. Ibid.

19. *The Nation*, 29 March 2008.

8

Conclusion: Rethinking Counter-Terrorism

As is apparent from the discussion in the last chapters, Saudi Arabia has chiselled the yardsticks of a credible domestic, regional and global counter-terrorism strategy. In the domestic sphere, the Kingdom's counter-terrorism approach is premised on a three-pronged strategy of prevention, cure, and care. Apart from adopting stringent security measures and legal procedures to fight, pre-empt and prevent terrorism, the Kingdom has undertaken wide-ranging reforms in the country's financial, banking, administrative, educational, information, and societal sectors as a means to finding a long lasting solution to the problem of terrorism. These include a host of steps aimed at fighting terrorism financing, and reforms in the curriculum being taught at educational institutions offering religious learning.

As the discussion in Chapters 5 and 6 make it clear, for those among the deviants who are arrested and jailed on charges of inciting or committing terrorism, the Saudi government has put in place an extensive 'out-reach' campaign, whereby religious scholars engage in a productive discourse with the detainees and their families, who are, likewise, taken care of. The government has also attempted to make former detainees responsible and useful citizens of the state by offering them incentives such as jobs and facilities for learning a variety of skills of their liking. The 'out-reach' campaign has produced positive results as many of the detainees suspected of inciting or committing terrorism, during their trial in court or the prison term, repented their past deeds and declared never to encourage terrorist activity, or take part in it.

The Saudi government has, likewise, been proactively engaged in bilateral and multilateral diplomacy to counter terrorism. For this purpose, it has cooperated with all countries, particularly the United States, and international organizations, especially the United Nations. It is also engaged in an ongoing strategic dialogue with the United States, with which it has also created a Joint Task Force against terrorist financing. The Saudi leadership has also floated the idea of setting up of an International Centre for Combating Terrorism under the auspices of the United Nations, through the February 2005 International Conference on Combating Terrorism in Riyadh as well as the December 2005 Extraordinary Summit of the OIC in Makkah.

It has also initiated a process of engagement by holding the Interfaith Dialogue, first at Makkah (4–6 June 2008) followed by the one in Madrid, Spain (16–18 July 2008) and then in New York (12–13 November 2008). King Abdullah bin Abdul Aziz inaugurated all these conferences stressing on the need for initiating an international dialogue among followers of various religions with the intention of forging harmony and understanding among them for a better and peaceful world. This would be a continuing process that is destined to make a major contribution in terms of vastly improving the prevalent environment for the followers of various religions and beliefs to be able to live together in peace as fellow citizens of the world.

A CONTEMPORARY PERSPECTIVE

The recent terrorist attacks on a hotel in Islamabad, Pakistan and on a number of targets in Mumbai, India have, once again, brought to the fore the need to tackle terrorism as a matter of urgency. It is here that the relevance of developing a credible strategy to fight the scourge assumes an even greater importance. Obviously, as stated earlier, the way forward is not through the use of force alone. It has to be complemented by other ingenious and practical initiatives that would help in influencing the mindset of those who may be engaged in the heinous acts.

On the other hand, the terrorism unleashed by Israel in Gaza recently is an apt reminder of the one-sidedness of the international perception and its inability to stop a state from using its brute power to subdue and terrorize people into subjugation. The state of Israel, in a show of blatant arrogance, has always been unwilling to comply with the United Nations resolutions and predominant international opinion calling for cessation of hostilities and initiation of steps that would contribute to the advent of an equitable and lasting peace in the Middle East, thus erasing one of the principal reasons behind the rationale for resorting to terrorism. On the other hand, the state of Israel has always taken measures to impose its own inhuman and unilateral will on a hapless people and perpetuate its terror at the expense of the inalienable right of self-expression of the people of Palestine. This is hardly an indication of progress on the road to eliminating terrorism from the world. A minimal reversal of this mindset is required even to initiate the movement towards the avowed goal.

It would also be appropriate to mention here the growing empowerment of non-state actors in conducting terrorist activities. These non-state actors are beyond the writ of the governments and are becoming increasingly powerful. The question arises as to who are funding them and helping them in training and provision of other wherewithal to undertake acts of terror? Steps need to be taken to create an all-encompassing strategy whereby the relevance of these supporters of terrorism that are funding the mechanism and acts of terror would be reduced appreciably over a period of time, and ultimately, they would be rendered totally ineffective. This cannot happen overnight and addressing the causes of terrorism would also be a critical factor in advancing a comprehensive solution for eliminating terrorism from across the world.

It is unfortunate that deviant forces in the world of Islam have come to the forefront of religious expression in the manner of terrorists, hijacking even genuine causes of Muslim liberation in the world. The US–Western questionable conduct *vis-à-vis* the Muslim world, based upon political duplicity including unduly backing Israel on Palestine and economic exploitation, may also have contributed to the radicalization of a section of the people in the Muslim world. While the international community cannot dispense with the use of military and non-military means to tackle the violent ramifications of terrorism, it also cannot overlook the larger political and economic causes which provide breeding grounds for religious hatred and radicalism, the rise of extremist movements, and fresh recruits for the bin Ladens of the world. It is only by duly addressing these causes that the current global wave of terrorism can be effectively reversed, and its potentially cataclysmic consequences avoided.

THE STRATEGY FOR GLOBAL ACTION AGAINST TERRORISM

It is a good omen that the US administration of President Barack Hussein Obama seems to realize the gravity of the current global crises, which cannot be addressed without a new, inclusive and multilateral approach on the part of the United States. The foremost challenge before President Obama is to restore America's image in the world that has seen an unprecedented deterioration in recent years, particularly in the Muslim world. President Obama's inaugural speech of 20 January 2009 carried a powerful, encouraging message to the Muslim world: that the United States seeks 'a new way forward based on mutual interest and mutual respect'. Within days, he delivered on this message, by ordering the closure of the infamous Guantánamo Bay prison and prohibiting torture of terror suspects in detention. Such radical steps, if combined with a more creative and cooperative US approach towards handling issues of extremism and terrorism, will have a lasting effect in reversing the course of the al-Qaeda-inspired international terrorist wave and improving America's image in the world, particularly in the Muslim countries facing the terrorist threat.

Only time will tell whether or when the US approach to world affairs moves away from the reckless employment of the use-of-force as a principal counter-terrorism option, as was the trend during the two-terms of the Bush administration, towards the use of 'smart power', as US Secretary of State Hillary Clinton stated during her Senate confirmation hearings, to reverse the course of international terrorism.

Broadly speaking, however, one must contend that international terrorism can be eliminated only through a common approach that is rigorously implemented by states in accordance with the principles and purposes of the Charter of the United Nations and international law, including humanitarian law and respect for human rights. The international community must commit itself to the prevention and elimination of terrorism by adopting multi-faceted measures. The states must come forth willingly in terms of fulfilling their obligation in the prevention and eradication of terrorism.

As part of their obligation to provide cooperation, states must take concrete action to eliminate terrorism by themselves. However, in view of the continuing tragic events relating to the scourge, the need to strengthen bilateral and international cooperation for combating it has further increased. Based on the principles that govern international cooperation in this area, additional measures could be adopted for immediate implementation to strengthen global action and the capacity of states to deal with these new threats.

While formulation of preventive laws at the domestic level remains a priority consideration, cooperation among states at the regional and international levels is no less important to combat the curse of terrorism. Therefore, a multi-pronged strategy incorporating various initiatives will provide a more effective means for eliminating terrorism from the face of the world. The problem of terrorism is not just confined to a few countries. It is an international phenomenon that has engulfed the world and a large number of countries have become a target of this menace. Over the last many years, Saudi Arabia has been a prime target of the terrorists. Combating terrorism requires international cooperation against terrorists from using territories of the countries in which they live as a springboard for their subversive activities. That is why it is the prime responsibility of all peace-loving states to pursue comprehensive action in the framework of international legitimacy to eradicate terrorism.

Enhanced cooperation and coordination among the countries of the world can make a considerable difference in terms of developing and implementing an effective approach to reduce and, eventually, eliminate terrorism from the world.

Force alone is not going to eliminate terrorism. It is a battle to win over hearts and minds. Terrorism is a heinous phenomenon. It has no place in Islam and is forbidden sternly, completely and without any ambiguity. Based on Islamic principles, the Saudi government has taken several strategic measures to counter terrorism, which have yielded positive results through the years.

In addition to governments of the world taking internal measures, it remains a foregone conclusion that the most critical aspect of the cumulative effort to combat terrorism successfully will be to eliminate its breeding grounds wherever those may be located. In this context, a dispassionate distinction will have to be made between the 'genuine will of the people of an area' and 'terrorist pursuits'. In the wake of the 11 September attacks in the United States, pursuits that, for decades, were recognized as 'freedom struggles' in some areas of the world are now erroneously being dubbed as 'terrorist activities'. At the same time, inalienable rights are being denied to some peoples while others continue to be subjected to untold brutalities and misery. This must not be allowed to continue and those countries that are responsible for such situations should be urged to come to agreement in consonance with the enshrining principles as enunciated by the United Nations from time to time. Without a swift extermination of these breeding grounds through a sincere and combined international effort, elimination of terrorism will remain a distant dream.

Extermination of terrorism is a game of winning over people—the ones who are the existing or potential perpetrators as well as those who may have suffered or who may be the potential targets of such heinous acts. While the former have to be convinced to distance themselves from further indulgence in undertaking dastardly acts of terrorism, the latter have to become proactive partners in the ultimate objective of exterminating this scourge from the world. It must be understood that terrorists cannot be bombed out of the face of the world. You kill ten, and another ten, even twenty, would be there to take their place. They have to be convinced that what they are doing is evil and against whatever faith they may hail from. Terrorism is a crime against humanity and no religion of the world, least of all Islam, permits its followers to kill other innocent human beings. Life is sacrosanct. No human being has the right to take it away. They must know this. They must understand this. They must honour this.

Concurrently, the international community should also concentrate on removing the genuine grievances that various people of the world may have suffered from, or may still be suffering from. Such breeding grounds have to be eliminated if the international community is to come to grips with the ultimate objective of combating and eliminating the scourge of terrorism from the world.

For any counter-terrorism measure to be successful, it should be comprehensive, both in the sense of attacking at all possible levels of operation as well as in terms of thoroughness at each level. It will not serve to eliminate terrorism if only the perpetrators are caught and sent to jail, while their financiers and facilitators are roaming the streets free, planning to bring further harm to mankind. Therefore, together with pursuing a short-term strategy in terms of destroying all avenues that are potentially dangerous, a comprehensive and well thought-out long-term strategy should also be put in place to combat and eliminate the scourge of terrorism. It is only through an effective combination of the two that the world may, some day, see the back of terrorism and escape the devastating consequences of this scourge.

IN PURSUIT OF A WORLD FREE OF TERROR

Critical to the war against terrorism is the cohesion among all countries of the world in a determined bid to uproot the evil. This can only happen if an equitable and legitimate basis exists for the same in the shape of an understanding of what affects a large number of people in the world in terms of their deprivation of basic rights as well as their access to opportunities for education, jobs, social elevation, and empowerment. Indeed, these are serious issues that would continue to plague the advance towards formulating an effective strategy for successful pursuit of the ultimate goal.

It is common understanding that opportunities cannot be created for some people by depriving others of the same, or basic rights and social freedoms granted to some by denying the same to others. No discrimination should be practised in providing an enabling ground for all people of the world to pursue their legitimate dreams. It is in the denial of these basic human rights to a vast section of the world population wherein we can see the germs of deviant thinking.

While force remains an option, it is not the means to eliminate terrorist thinking or pursuits. The solution lies in forging a close and workable understanding among the players engaged in the pursuit of eliminating this scourge based on a recognition of the inalienable rights of the people of the world without any prejudice on the basis of caste, colour or creed. It is also linked with following a policy of education and reform as part of the way the authorities approach the malaise.

Saudi Arabia has succeeded in putting all the critical pieces together by formulating a viable and proactive policy suited to its culture and environment with regard to tackling the cancer of terrorism. It has shown ample signs of working successfully within the country while others have also shown an interest in emulating the Saudi strategy to tackle terror in their midst. The Saudi model is a mix of ingenious steps that are relevant to its society and its demands while it contains all the ingredients of an effective approach that can easily be adapted by other countries of the world.

In the pursuit of combating terrorism, it must be kept in mind that while one may learn from strategies followed by other countries, in the end, it has to be an indigenous and home grown strategy that would work. While there may be obvious similarities in the obtaining situations in two different countries that may encourage the leaders to borrow from each other, there would also be obvious dissimilarities that would discourage a process of blindly emulating all the contours of a strategy. A more workable recipe would be to adapt the principal yardsticks to the home needs of another country and mix them with the local requirements for optimum results.

It only goes to show that, given the will and determination, and sensitivity to the genuine concerns of inequity and deprivation of the people of the world, the war against terror can be pursued and won. After all, it remains a war that is critical to the very survival of humankind and its values.

Bibliography

Ahmad, Ishtiaq. 'Karen Armstrong on Islamic Legacy of Compassion.' *Weekly Pulse.* 8–14 February 2008.

Ahmad, Ishtiaq. 'Indonesia's Counter-Terrorism Success: Lessons for Pakistan's Fight against Terrorism.' In Area Study Centre for Far East and Southeast Asia, ed. *Enhancing Pakistan–Indonesia Relations: Perspectives and Challenges.* Jamshoro, Pakistan: University of Sindh, 2008.

Ahmad, Ishtiaq. 'Religious Terrorism.' In Palmer Fernandez, ed. *Encyclopaedia of Religion and War.* New York: Berkshire/Routledge, 2003.

Ahmad, Ishtiaq. 'Repenting and Recanting Religious Radicalism.' *Weekly Pulse.* 23–29 May 2008.

Ahmad, Ishtiaq. 'Simplifying a Complex Issue: The Problem in Understanding Terrorism.' Paper presented at a conference on 'Terrorism and Extremism: Social-Psychological Perspectives.' National Institute of Psychology, Quaid-i-Azam University. Islamabad, 15–17 October 2008.

Ahmad, Ishtiaq. 'The Organization of Islamic Conference: From Ceremonial Politics to Politicization?' In Harders and Legrenzi, eds. *Beyond Regionalism? Regional Cooperation, Regionalism and Regionalisation in the Middle East.* London: Ashgate, 2008.

Ahmad, Ishtiaq. 'West European Perceptions of Islam.' *Weekly Pulse*. 14–20 April 2006.

Ahmad, Ishtiaq. 'Why Islam Forbids Terrorism.' *Weekly Pulse*. 28 June–3 July 2008.

Al Madani, Abdullah. 'Indonesia's Success in Its War on Terror.' *Gulf News*. 1 July 2007.

Al-Mufarih, Ahmed S. *The Role of the Kingdom of Saudi Arabia in Combating Terrorism*. USAWC Strategy Research Project. Carlisle Barracks, Penn.: US Army War College, 3 May 2004.

Al Shafey, Mohammed. 'Egypt: Jailed Al-Qaeda Ideologue Urges Halt to Attacks Contradicting Islamic Law.' *Asharq Al-Awsat*. 8 May 2007. http://aawsat.com/english/news.asp?section=1andid=8894

Boucek, Christopher. *Saudi Arabia's 'Soft' Counter-Terrorism Strategy: Prevention, Rehabilitation and Aftercare*. Carnegie Papers. Washington, DC: Carnegie Endowment for International Peace, September 2008.

Boisard, Marcel A. *Jihad: A Commitment to Universal Peace*. Indianapolis: American Trust Publication 1988.

Brummitt, Chris. 'South-East Asia Beats Back Al-Qaeda.' *The Associated Press*. 10 October 2007.

Carter, Jimmy. *Palestine: Peace not Apartheid*. New York: Simon and Schuster, 2007.

Combs, Cynthia. *Terrorism in the Twenty-First Century*. New Jersey: Prentice Hall, 2003.

Cordesman, Anthony H. *Saudi Arabia Enters the Twenty-First Century: The Political, Foreign Policy, Economic, and Energy Dimensions.* Westport, Conn: Praeger, 2003.

Department of Defence. *Dictionary of Military and Associated Terms.* Joint Publication 1–02. Washington, DC: DOD, 2002.

Dillon, Dana R. 'Make Fighting Terrorism the First Priority.' *The Asian Wall Street Journal.* 20 October 2004.

Esposito, John. *Unholy War: Terror in the Name of Islam.* New York: Oxford University Press, 2002.

Fatany, Samar. 'Combating Terrorism and Extremism in Saudi Arabia. *Arab News.* 7 December 2004.

Friedman, Thomas L. 'Mandela Memo on Palestine.' *New York Times.* 28 March 2002.

Friedman, Thomas L. 'An Intriguing Signal from the Saudi Crown Prince.' *The New York Times.* 17 February 2002.

Guelke, Adrian. *The Age of Terrorism and the International Political System.* New York: St. Martin's Press, 1995.

Halawi, Jailan. 'Bidding Violence Farewell.' *Al-Ahram Weekly.* 22–28 November 2007. http://weekly.ahram.org.eg/2007/872/eg5.htm

Harmon, Christopher. *Terrorism Today.* London: Frank Cass, 1995.

Hoffman, Bruce. *Inside Terrorism.* New York: Columbia University Press, 1999.

Huntington, Samuel P. 'The Age of Muslim Wars,' *Newsweek,* December 2001–January 2002.

Huntington, Samuel P. *The Clash of Civilizations and the Remaking of World Order*. New York: Simon and Schuster, 1996.

Initiatives and Actions Taken by the Kingdom of Saudi Arabia in the War on Terrorism. Washington, DC: Royal Embassy of Saudi Arabia, December 2006. www.saudiembassy.net

Juergensmeyer, Mark. *Terror in the Mind of God: The Global Rise of Religious Violence*. Berkeley: University of California Press, 2001.

Kurlantzick, Joshua. 'How Indonesia is Winning its War on Terror.' *Time Magazine*. 9 August 2007.

Kurlantzick, Joshua. Where the War on Terror is Succeeding.' *Commentary*. Carnegie Endowment for International Peace, May 2007.

Kushner, Harvey W. 'Suicide Bombers: Business as Usual.' *Studies in Conflict and Terrorism*. Vol. 19, 1996.

Laqueur, Walter. *No End to War: Terrorism in the Twenty-First Century*. New York: The Continuum International Publishing Group, 2003.

Laqueur, Walter. *The New Terrorism*. New York: Oxford University Press, 1999.

MacFarquhar, Neil. 'Al Qaeda Blamed in Deadly Attack on Saudi Homes.' *The New York Times*. 10 November 2003.

Maley, William. *Fundamentalism Reborn: Afghanistan and the Taliban*. London: C. Hurst and Co., 1998.

Malik, Sajjad. 'Afghan, Iraq Wars have Fuelled Terrorism, Violence: Asseri.' *Daily Times*. 5 May 2008.

Merari, A. 'The Readiness to Kill and Die: Suicidal Terrorism in the Middle East.' In W. Reich, ed., *Origins of Terrorism: Psychologies, Ideologies, Theologies and States of Mind*. New York, Cambridge University Press, 1998.

'OIC Summit to Seek Moderate Islam Image after Terror Attacks.' *Agence France Presse*, 5 December 2005.

Owen, Richard, 'Saudi King Calls for Interfaith Talks,' *Time Magazine*, 25 March 2008.

Palti, Leslie. 'Combating Terrorism while Protecting Human Right.' *UN Chronicle*, Vol. XLI. 4 November 2004.

Payne, Carroll. 'Reasons behind Terrorism.' *Global Terrorism*. March 2002. http://www.glopbalterrorism101.com/ReasonsBehindTerrorism.html

Pillar, Paul R. *Terrorism and US Foreign Policy*. Washington, DC: Brookings Institute Press, 2001.

Post-September 11 Scenarios: The Efforts of the Embassy of Saudi Arabia, Pakistan, to Combat Terrorism. Islamabad: Embassy of the Kingdom of Saudi Arabia, 2005.

'Powers of Persuasion.' *The Economist*. 17 July 2008.

Ressa, Maria. *Seeds of Terror: An Eyewitness Account of Al-Qaeda's Newest Center of Operations in Southeast Asia*. New York: Free Press, 2003.

Rhanem, Karima. 'Challenges Facing OIC Summit.' *Morocco Times*. 12 December 2005.

Rizvi, Hasan-Askari. 'Theoretical Formulations on Terrorism.' In Institute of Regional Studies. *Global Terrorism: Genesis, Implications, Remedial and Counter-Measures*. Islamabad: PanGraphics, 2006.

Rudolph, Rachael M. *Saudi Arabia's War on Terrorism: From 1929 to 2003*. VDM Verlag, 2009.

Saudi Arabia and the Fight against Terrorist Financing. Testimony of J. Cofer Black, Coordinator for Counterterrorism, US Department of State, to the Middle East and Central Asia Subcommittee of the House International Relations Committee, 24 March 2004.

Schmid, Alex. 'The Response Problem as a Definition Problem.' *Terrorism and Political Violence*. Vol. 4, No. 4. 1992.

Schmid, Alex, et al. *Political Terrorism*. New Jersey: Transaction, 1988.

Shipler, David K. *Arab and Jew: Wounded Spirits in a Promised Land*. New York: Penguin, 1987.

Stern, Jessica. *The Ultimate Terrorists*. Cambridge: Harvard University Press, 2001.

Stracke, Nicole. 'Arab Prisons: A Place for Dialogue and Reform.' *Perspectives on Terrorism*. Vol. 1, No. 4, 2007.

Talbott, Strobe and Nayan Chanda. *The Age of Terror: America and the World after September 11*. New York: Basic Books, 2001.

The Holy Quran. Surah 2: Verses 148, 190, 192, 205, 256 and 294; Surah 4, Verses 90 and 93; Surah 5, Verses 11, 33 and 34 Surah 8, Verse 61; Surah 9, Verses 5, 29 and 91; Surah 22, Verse 39 and 67; Surah 28, Verse 77; Surah 47, Verse 4; Surah 48, Verse 17; Surah 49, Verse 1. Translation by Dr Muhammad Taqi-ud-din al-Hilali and Dr Muhammad

Muhsin Khan, King Fahad Complex for the printing of the Holy Qur'an, Madinah, Saudi Arabia, 8 February 2001.

Tollitz, N.P. ed. *Saudi Arabia, US Relations and Oil*. Nova Science Publishers, Inc, 2005.

Townshend, Charles. *Terrorism: A Very Short Introduction*. Oxford: Oxford University Press, 2002.

Trofimov, Yaroslav. *The Siege of Mecca: The Forgotten Uprising*. New York: Penguin, 2007.

Weinberg, Leonard. *Global Terrorism: A Beginner's Guide*. Oxford: Oneworld Publications, 2006.

White, John. *Terrorism: An Introduction*. Belmont, CA: Wadsworth, 2002.

Worth, Robert F. 'Saudis Retool to Root Out Terrorist Risk.' *The New York Times*. 21 March 2009.

Index